The universe
has always
off-balance
itself out :-)

all the time
I cried over you,
all the times
I laughed with you...
They even out
Love is a
zero sum game.
Try we can't say

Happiness
The Delight-Tree

An Anthology of Contemporary
International Poetry

In honour of the International Day of Happiness

Happiness
The Delight-Tree

An Anthology of Contemporary International Poetry

Edited by Bhikshuni Weisbrot
Darrel Alejandro Holnes
Elizabeth Lara

UNITED SOCIETY
NATIONS SRC OF WRITERS

ISBN: 9781938599729

Editors:
Bhikshuni Weisbrot, Darrel Alejandro Holnes, Elizabeth Lara
Designed and printed by The Manifestation Glow Press
Designer: Shantishri McGrath
President: Abakash Konopiaty

Printed in the United States of America
First Edition–Second Printing
April 2015

United Nations SRC Society of Writers
c/o Bhikshuni Weisbrot, President
165-20 Chapin Court, Jamaica, New York 11432
Visit our website at http://www.unsrcsocietyofwriters.org/

FOREWORD

Are you courageous?
Then prove it to me
With your unparalleled
Happiness.

Sri Chinmoy

Twenty-Seven Thousand
Aspiration-Plants, Part 166

Inspired by the Kingdom of Bhutan and its successful implementation of an innovative policy of Gross National Happiness, the United Nations in 2012 perceived the wisdom of promoting happiness as a personal and societal goal towards which the world family could advantageously strive.

Following an initial meeting on the topic in 2012, the UN gathered and published research on well-being from experts in a wide range of fields including economics, business, psychology, sociology, political science and education. Using recognized indicators, they were able to illustrate in practical ways how to identify and expand the genuine happiness that has sustained, transformed and elevated humanity throughout history.

Although indicators differed, it was unanimously agreed that the pursuit of happiness far transcends pleasure-seeking, and that a deeper inner happiness embraces such values as service, love, community, relationship, health and self-mastery, as well as freedom and economic stability.

Many of these values were given poetic expression by Sri Chinmoy, founder of the Peace Meditation at the United Nations, who wrote hundreds of poems on the subject of happiness that served as the inspiration for this collection. In tribute, we dedicate and close the anthology with his poetry. Building on his work by seeking to collect and generate more "poetry of happiness" seemed the most fitting way for the

United Nations SRC Society of Writers to celebrate the International Day of Happiness (20 March), so declared by UN General Assembly Resolution 66/281

The project began with letters to the Permanent Missions to the United Nations of those countries that had strongly supported General Assembly Resolution 65/309, entitled "Happiness: Towards a Holistic Approach to Development." But it quickly expanded, through the support of a number of these Missions, to literary organizations, festivals and poetry networks worldwide, resulting in a collection of happiness poetry that represents 56 countries and 31 languages. We are grateful to the Permanent Missions for their enthusiastic response.

These poems are the generous self-offering of both renowned and emerging poets worldwide. They strongly affirm that the pursuit of happiness is our universal birthright. It is our hope that this first volume will serve to inspire more poetry of happiness, and that the International Day of Happiness will become an annual occasion to showcase and celebrate new creative works and collaborations. We invite you to join us in our aspiration to bring more happiness into the world, and we welcome you to our Delight-Tree.

Bhikshuni Weisbrot
President, United Nations SRC Society of Writers

ACKNOWLEDGEMENTS

The editors would like to express their appreciation to the Permanent Missions of the States Members of the United Nations, whose support was crucial in reaching out to the poets who appear in the present collection. Special thanks are owed to the following: H. E. Mr. Kaha Imnadze, Ambassador, Permanent Representative of Georgia to the United Nations; Mrs. Inga Kanchaveli, Counsellor, Permanent Mission of Georgia to the United Nations; Mr. Matej Marn, Counsellor, Deputy Permanent Representative, Permanent Mission of Slovenia to the United Nations; and Ms. Petra Yliportimo, First Secretary, Permanent Mission of Finland to the United Nations. The following people, offices and organizations have contributed their time, energy and expertise to this effort: Chidi Achebe; Mohammed Al-Jabir; Nora Atalla; Asmaa Awad-Farid; June Ban, Permanent Mission of the Republic of Korea to the United Nations; Lea Banks; Tanima Bossart; Cheryl Boyce-Taylor; Suchana Cao; Eduardo C. Corral; Ram Devineni; Rajnandini Paula Flood; Nemi Fredner; Ranjana Ghose; Celeste Guzman Mendoza; Saujanya B. Gzela; Prakhara Harter; Nayana Hein; Geoffrey Fitzgibbon Hughes; Sehwa Jang; Pujarini Guðný Jónsdóttir; Tomoyo Kamimura, Director, Language Education and Library, and Tiffany Ferentini, Librarian, Japan Society; George Keefer; Bhadra Kleinman; Hélène Lepine; Khaled Mattawa; Parvati McPheeters; Shinja Møller; Apara Heloisa Monnerat; Maureen Moore; Iurii Moskalev; Mahatapa Palit; Pragati Pascale; Sweta Pradhan; Sukham Rodrigues; Estefania Samper; Robyn Sauer; Nilima Silver; Sanyogita Sisler; Harashita Sunaoshi; United Nations Bookshop; United Nations Department of Public Information, Outreach Division, NGO Relations, Advocacy & Special Events, Creative Community Outreach Initiative, Messenger of Peace Programme; Sladjana Vracar; Sharika Maria Xavier; Jeffrey Yang; Abdulrahman Zaza and Di Zou. We are grateful for the expert advice we received from our printer and designer at the Manifestation Glow, Abakash Konopiaty and Shantishri McGrath. Finally, we honour all the poets whose work appears in this volume. We share their words in the belief that our readers will find in them, as we have, hope, joy, love, and the myriad paths to happiness.

CONTENTS

NORTH AMERICA

Canada

United States of America

OCEANIA

Australia

Closing / 174

Biographies / 175

Credits / 193

INTRODUCTORY NOTE

Every widely spoken language has a word for happiness, and the poets who appear in *Happiness: The Delight Tree – An Anthology of Contemporary International Poetry*, have found a multitude of ways to express their understanding of that feeling. They explore ideas as diverse as nature, well-being, family, love, faith, history, language, and politics. Despite the many cultural and historical differences between the literary traditions at the heart of each poet's work, the anthology harmonizes their diversity; taken together, their work is a celebration of what it truly means to be happy.

In the anthology, the poets show readers that happiness can be both that which is stumbled upon and that which is pursued and discovered, as in *How to be Happy in 101 Days*, where Indian poet Tishani Doshi writes that to find happiness one must, "Use the knife lustily: to peel the mango's/jealous skin, to wean bark and cut bread/for the unending hunger of stray dogs". For the German poet Gernot Blume, happiness is less about action or interaction and more about perspective. His poem Light tells us, "The search for happiness/needs favorable lighting/to cast short shadows." Perhaps Syrian poet Adonis agrees with Blume, as his poem *Tomorrow* speaks of a world blanketed in light, where "wherever I look/the world is my field of play."

But what about those moments when happiness just seems to appear? What about moments in which serendipity and surprise delightfully interrupt banality or tragedy? For this we turn to Marjorie Evasco from the Philippines, who writes in *Third World Music on the 23rd Day of Rain*, "Roof leaks, still falls rain./My pots and pans fill, half-full/With monsoon music." After such a precious and sudden moment of joy amidst floods in the Philippines, we may find ourselves in Poland, where Zofia Beszczyńska writes that happiness is "a sudden moment of light/in the dark/movement of the wind in the white sky."

Yet for all the moments where happiness takes us by surprise there are moments when it is earned by daring or cunning, by making the harder choice. In his poem *In a Tent on the Tundra*, Canadian poet Jean Désy writes, "People daring to talk about harmony/When everywhere in the world/There is so much impatience." Happiness also comes from hard choices: Russian Federation poet Yevgeny Yevtushenko, in his poem *Divine Happiness*, writes, "Divine Happiness knocks on your door/When you choose not to go to war."

Wherever you find happiness or wherever it may find you, these poets will remind you that once it's there you can celebrate. Discovering happiness in song, Yusef Komunyakaa of the United States of America writes, in his poem *With My Fish-Skin Drum*, "I shall sing the caravan home again,/bone & muscle holding me together,/earth & sky beneath my feet." The celebration continues with blessings in Salvadorian poet Javier Zamora's poem *Si Fuera*, "Bless/the drought of bullets, cured cholera, and the comfort/of earthquakes."

The editors recognize that anthologies are different things to different people; *Happiness: The Delight-Tree* has been compiled as a portable library of poems to honour the International Day of Happiness. Here, the reader will find works by international poets from a variety of literary backgrounds, some well-established in their nations and beyond, and others who are emerging or amateur poets. Despite their differing backgrounds, they have in common a verse and lyric that challenges and encourages readers in the pursuit of their own happiness. We hope that this is a library that you will want to carry with you, and consult again and again.

Secretary-General Ban Ki-Moon, in his message for the International Day of Happiness 2014, said "Happiness may have different meanings for different people. But we can all agree that it means working to end conflict, poverty and other unfortunate conditions in which so many of our fellow human beings live." Whether happiness is stumbled upon, discovered, earned, serendipitous or celebrated, in this anthology it is expressed by poets from around the world as their testament to its place in the human story and its necessity in the human experience.

Darrel Alejandro Holnes   *and*   Elizabeth Lara
Poet & Editor   *Poet & Editor*

Dedication

The Roots of Delight-Tree

Every human being
In his soul's progress-march
Will ultimately discover
The roots of delight-tree
That weave and unweave
Through the earth-bound life.

–Sri Chinmoy

AFRICA

Photo: Adarini Inkei

|| *Cabo Verde* ||

David Hopffer Almada

Um Dia Feliz

O mar acordou
Sereno e calmo
E mais azul
Muito mais azul!
Os peixes
Que o povoam
Saltitam
Empertigados
Quais dançarinos
Sobre as ondas!

O céu também
Está mais azul...
Nem uma nuvem
Tolda o sol
Que, sereno e radioso,
Passeia, lentamente,
Lá em cima!

As plantas
Cá em baixo
Mais verdes
Mais viçosas estão
E as flores
Mais coloridas
Surgem
De vermelho e amarelo
Vestidas
A todos brindando
Com a suavidade
Do seu perfume!

David Hopffer Almada

A Happy Day

The sea woke up
Serene and calm
And more blue
Much more blue!
The fish
Hop like dancers
On the waves!

The sky as well
Is more blue...
Not even a cloud
Covers the sun,
Serene and radiant –
Pacing slowly,
Above!

The plants
Here below are
More green
More lush
And the flowers
Dressed in red and yellow
More colorful,
Toasting to all
With the gentleness
Of their perfume!

Even the birds
Come together
Fluttering about
Dedicating

Até as aves
Se juntam
Esvoaçando por ai
E dedicando
Numa suave melodia
Um hino inedito
A este dia claro
E luminoso...

Os populares
De vestes garridas
De repente assomam
E desfilam
Pelas ruas da Cidade
Ao som de tambores
Numa grande miscelânea
De sons e ritmos
-Ferro/gaita/violão/cavaquinho
Simboa/reco-reco/violino
Morna/coladeira/funaná
Batuque/kolá sanjon
Mazurka/talaia baixon/landun
Numa inolvidável
Serenata matinal!

E o dia vai correndo
Rapidamente escorrendo
Em festa e na sabura...

Tudo está
Mais sorridente
Mais radiante
Mais vivo!

Tudo parece
Mais feliz!

Afinal
E cinco de Julho
Um dia especial
Um DIA FELIZ!

In a sweet melody
An unpublished hymn
To this clear
And bright day.

Suddenly
The people
In lively garments
Appear
And parade
In the streets of the City
To the sound of drums,
In a great medley
Of sounds and rhythms
– Ferro/gaita/violao/cavaquinho
Simboa/reco-reco/violino
Morna/coladeira/funana
Batuque/kola sanjon
Mazurka/talaia baixon/landun*
– An unforgettable
Morning serenade!

And the day runs quickly
Overflowing
With party spirit
And in the *sabura*

Everything is
Smiling
Radiant
More alive!

Everything looks
Happier!

At last
It's the fifth of July**
A special day
A HAPPY DAY!

Translated from Portuguese by Silas Pinto.
* Names of musical instruments in Cabo Verdean Kriolu.
** On the 5th of July, Cabo Verde gained independence after
  500 years of Portuguese rule.

Iman Mersal

في كامل فرحهـم

سأُدخل التليفون إلى سريري

وأُحدّثهم قبل النوم في أمورٍ كثيرة،

لأتأكّد أنهـم موجودون بالفِعل

وأن لديهم مواعيدَ لنهاية الأسبوع،

وأماناً

يجعلهم يخافون من الشيخوخة

ويكذبون أحياناً.

سأتأكّد أنهم موجودون بالفعل

في كامِل فرحِهـم

وأنني وحدي

وأن الصباحَ ممكنٌ

طالما هناك أحقادٌ جديدة.

Iman Mersal

In Perfect Happiness

Before I sleep
I will take the phone to bed
and talk to them about many things,
make sure they are really there,
that they have dates for the weekend,
and enough security
to make them fear old age
and make them lie.

I will make sure they are really there
in perfect happiness,
and that I am alone
and that the morning is possible
as long as there are fresh resentments.

Translated from Arabic by Khaled Mattawa.

‖ *Ghana* ‖

Abena P.A. Busia

A Wedding Song

For Chic Streetman and Karen Sorenson
on their Wedding Day, October 2nd, 1993

This is your first song together.

As with certain voices you claim
a sudden love
making peace with solitary pasts
to walk together
into the mystery of a future
forever bound

Remember – a future forever bound
is a rugged path forever blessed;
for marriage is the first rite
of miracles of human faith,
its vows our unique and sacred songs

And to be surprised by love
is to be caressed
by the sudden touch of God.

Kwame Dawes

Charged
After G.M. Hopkins

To see the grandeur, my eyes must filter out the ordinary,
the dross of ingratitude, the dregs of dull skepticism

and the cynic's wit, and replace it all with the base
humility of laughter, gratitude, the ability to say

while strolling uphill against a wind-chill's sudden
bite, look, look, look at my breath rising in clouds into

the brittle air, look at the way the sun slashes across
the snow; feel the grip of traction of my warm boots,

rejoice in the snugness of gloves, the shelter of scarves–
how grand is the brilliance of ice hanging from trees!

Ikeogu Oke

N'ihi Gị

N'ihi gị a ga m n'akpọ ọja oku
Ịfụ opi aṅụrị m;
A ga m n'akpọ ekwe oku
Iti mkpu ọṅụ m.

Ị bịakwutere m dịka ngọzi
Egwuchiri egwuchi.
Mana ihe ngwuchi ahụ a dịzighị;
Nanị ngọzi ahụ fọdụrụ.

N'ihi gị, a ga m n'akpọ udu n'akpọ ogele
Ka ha bịa soro m ṅụrịa;
A ga m n'akpọ elu na ala ka ha bịa gba aka ebe,
Na obi dị m ụtọ.

N'ihi gị, n'eziokwu n'ihi gị,
A ga m n'aga ije sekelem sekelem
Ka onye ihu ọma kpọrọ,
Maka na abụ m onye ihu ọma kpọrọ!

Ikeogu Oke

For Your Sake

For your sake, I shall call upon the flute
To sing my joy;
I shall call upon the wooden gong
To proclaim my pleasure.

You came to me like a blessing
In disguise.
Now the disguise is no more;
Only the blessing remains.

For your sake, I shall call upon the clay drum and the
    metal gong
To come and rejoice with me;
I shall call upon the earth and the sky to come and
    bear witness,
That I am happy.

For your sake, truly for your sake,
I shall walk with grace and delicacy*
Like one made fortunate,
For I am indeed fortunate!

Translated from Igbo by Ikeogu Oke.
·The names of some of the Igbo musical instruments and the phrase,
"with grace and delicacy," which is a translation of "sekelem sekelem"
(an Igbo coinage by the poet), are semantic approximations.

|| *South Africa* ||

Gabeba Baderoon

Primal Scene

The murmur of my father and mother
in their bedroom down the passage,
her soft, private laugh.

Kirsten Holmes

I Am

I am the God-Woman.
I dance a universe
and my wrists erase the stars.
I am the effigy.

I have conquered despair.
Despair grieves everything
therefore I have conquered everything.

I am the God-Woman.
I line my eyes with Mars dust
and gloss my lips with moon-glow.

I am the God-Woman.
I am. I am. I am.

Natalia Molebatsi

i wish you...happy

i wish you whole
as words watering a flower
beneath the yellow rays of yearnings
beyond the reach of growling pains
i wish you inviolable dreams
flourishing under the
silent and attentive gaze of the moon
i wish you a sky,
open enough and ready
for thoughts of light
simple earthly delights
pouring in and out of this moment
i wish you alive
playing a game of cards
in the blossoming
pathway of unfolded wings
here, a wish for you,
of brave dreamlings
touching your eyes at dawn
picking shells along the beach with your brother
on the roof of your home, feeding doves
fitting your wedding gown
marvelling at the beat of your sister's heart
laughing at your father's funny stories
happy...
harvesting olives and memories

ASIA

Photo: Unmesh Swanson

|| *Bangladesh* ||

Nazmun Nesa Piari

বৃষ্টি

বৃষ্টি নেচে উঠবে
ঘাগরা পরা
জিপসি মেয়ের মত।
তুমি আমায় চুম্বন দিতে দিতে বললে,
বৃষ্টির দিন এলো বলে।

বৃষ্টি পড়বে উৎসবের বাসনকোসনের মতো।
বৃষ্টি পড়বে ঢাকায়,
বৃষ্টি পড়বে পাগলায়।
বৃষ্টি পড়বে ইখলাসপুরে,
বৃষ্টি পড়বে ঘরের ভেতরে।

বৃষ্টি পড়বে নদীর ঢেউয়ে
বৃষ্টি পড়বে মাছের শরীরে
বৃষ্টি পড়বে ঝিনুকের গায়ে
বৃষ্টি পড়বে কাঁটাতারে আর কংক্রিটের দেয়ালে—
বৃষ্টি পড়বে গোলাপের শরীরে।

বৃষ্টি পড়বে পুরানা পল্টনে,
বৃষ্টি পড়বে আমার কৈশোরে।
বৃষ্টি পড়বে আমার যৌবনে,
বৃষ্টি পড়বে এয়ারপোর্টে।

বৃষ্টির দিনে প্রেমিকের লক্ষ লক্ষ চুম্বন
শুধু আমার ওপরে ঝরে পড়বে।

Nazmun Nesa Piari

Waiting for Rain

Dancing like a gypsy girl in skirts
The rain will come.

The rain will come, you say.
I kiss and say yes,
The rain will come.

The rain will fall like a festival,
  Will fall in Dhaka
   Fall in Pagla
    In Ikhlaspur
    In the room.

The rain will fall on the South Pole
   Under the river
   On the swan's back
   On the fish.

The rain will fall in Purana Paltan
   Will fall on my teens
   On my youth.

The rain will fall on the airport.

In the season of rainy days
Millions of kisses will rain
   On me.

Translated from Bengali by Rakshat Puri.

‖ *China* ‖

Di Zou

素歌

我在夜雨中行走
没有伞
也不用缩起脖子
空气清凉
偶尔一阵芳香

有什么东西
随尘土落下
人心更安定些了

城市是开心的
车轮慢下
有轻轻的沙沙的响

我哼起小调
看墨色柏油路面
泛起温柔的光

Di Zou

Plain Song

I walk in the evening rain
No umbrella
No need
To raise my shoulders
Air is cool
An occasional fragrance

Something settled
With the dust
Men's heart
Is more sure

The city is happy
Wheels slowed down
Rustling in peace

I hum a small tune
See black road
Bathed in soft light

Translated from Mandarin by Di Zou.

Nora Nadjarian

Wanderlust

On the landing between two floors
the air hangs scented with fruits and bats.
I press my face against those dark smells,
climb the staircase, feeling the rough wall
with my palms all the way to the equator.

Behind the door is another continent, and you.

‖ *India* ‖

Tishani Doshi

How to be Happy in 101 Days

Resist stone. Learn to manoeuvre
against the heat of things. Should
you see butterflies gambol in the air,
resist the urge to pinch their wings.
Look for utilitarian values of violence.
Use the knife lustily: to peel the mango's
jealous skin, to wean bark and cut bread
for the unending hunger of stray dogs.
Renounce your house. Take just one
object with you. Slip it in your pocket.
Marvel at how a simple thing can
connect the variegated skeins of time.
On the 99th day, you must surrender
this object, but until then feel free
to attach sentiment to it. Find a forest
to disappear in. Look for thirst-quenching
plants. Rub the smooth globes of their roots
in your palms before biting into their hearts.
Lean backwards and listen to the slippery
bastard of your own arrhythmic heart.
Remind yourself that you feel pain,
therefore you must be alive. Stain
your fingers with ink. Set out into
the world and prepare to be horrified.
Do not close your eyes. Catch a fish.
Smash its head and watch the life gasp
out of it. Spit the bones into sand.
Offer your bones to someone.

Clavicles are the chief seducers
of the human body. When you hear
the snap, allow yourself a shudder.
Find a tree to hold all the faces
of your dead—their hair, their rings.
Hang their solemn portraits from branches.
If you cannot find happiness in death
you will not complete the course.
Give your child to a stranger.
If you are childless, offer the person
you love best. Do not ask about possible
ways of mistreatment. Trust it will be terrible.
Climb a mountain. Feel how much larger
the world is when you're alone. Think
of your child. Try to find words or images
to explain your loss. Give up. Stand on your head.
Grow dizzy on your own blood.
Spend the night in a cemetery.
Keep still and listen to the dead chortle.
Tattoo your face. Do not bother with stars.
They are for romantics (who are not happy
people). Learn to steer through darkness.
If you're attacked, spread your legs and say,
Brother, why are you doing this to me?
When you approach a crossing in the woods,
take the one instinct tells you to take.
When you are knee-deep in mud turn
around and try the other path in order
to understand how little you know
of yourself. In a few days you'll be ready
for the sublime. Before that, meditate
in a cave. If a tigress finds you offer her

the meat of your thighs, give her cubs
your breasts. If tigers are already extinct,
wait for some other hairy, hungry creature
to accost you. It will happen.
It is important for you to lose both
body and mind. Dig a hole in the earth
with your hands. Place your treasured
object in it and thrill at how little
it means to let it go. On the 101st
day, search out a mirror. Strip
away your clothes. Inch up to
your reflection. Much of the success
of this course will depend on what you see.

Anjum Hasan

In My Mother's Clothes

I feel the cool sweat from under my arms
soak her blouse timidly – shy, damp flowers
of my sweat on her blouse.

I wear her thirst blue and forest green
and burnt orange as if they belonged to me:
my mother's colours on my skin
in a dusty city.

I walk in her clothes
laughing inside, relieved
of the burden of being what one wears
since in my mother's clothes
I am neither myself nor my mother,

but more like that spindly
creature of six who slips onto
her fingers her mother's gold rings,
pulls on a huge cardigan that smells of sunlight and milk,
and conducts herself, drowsy with love, through rooms
with their curtains drawn against the honeyed light of June.

Sunil Sharma

Flowers in a Pot

The slim widower
Tends daily to the potted plants;
His specialty the white flowers
In a corner of the balcony
Of the one-room apartment
On the eleventh floor,
In the heart of the commercial district.
From that vantage point, the world is a blur
And nobody cares for the grumpy man,
Nor he, for them,
He is so bitter;
But, flowers beckon, dancing in the wind,
And the muttering occupant, lonely and miserable,
Waters them daily and they both talk,
And he sees in their smiling
Tender petals,
A son now forever lost;
These brief conversations
Conducted twice, everyday
Delight an ageing heart.
Through fragrance and colour,
The long-stemmed flowers,
Fragile and vulnerable,
Spread cheer everywhere,
Every nook and corner,
Like the sunflowers of
Van Gogh.

|| *Islamic Republic of Iran* ||

Mimi Khalvati

The Robin and the Eggcup

A robin flew into my room today,
into the sun of it, the wood, the plants.

A robin flew into my sleep today,
once for mischief, twice for very good luck.

A robin flew into my soul today,
queried it, rose and flumped against its glass.

So I opened it and the cold came in,
I levered it wide and the bird flew out.

Not for the first time. I let it out too,
my son said, out of the kitchen window.

No! When? Earlier, when you were asleep.
It broke an eggcup. Eggcup! What eggcup?

Not one of those nice blue and white eggcups.
Yes, he said joyfully, I swept it up.

Shirin Razavian

گویی که کودکی‌ام را . . .

خوشه‌های شادمانی‌ام آه
شاداب‌تر ز خوشه‌ی انگورند
با قطره‌های شبنم خوش قلبی
گویی که کودکی‌ام را
دوباره می‌زیم

هر چیز تازه است
و بوی تازگی دارد
و در هر گوشه اتاقم
امید می‌روید
و از درزهای پنجره‌ام رشته‌های ماه
به داخل خزیده‌اند

من غنچه‌های غم انگیز جنگ را
ناچار چیده‌ام
مبادا که بشکفند
و اشکدان خویش را
که شیشه عمر دیو اندوه است
از صخره‌های گذشته به پائین فکنده‌ام
و سیاهی را دریده‌ام
تا خون سپیدش صفحه‌ی حیات را فرا بگیرد

فقر و گرسنگی را
در صف دردهای درمان پذیر گذاشته‌ام
که باید دوا شوند
گرسنگی را تکه نانی می‌کشد
و با فقر هم می‌توان شادمان بود
یک روز همه دردها را دوا خواهم کرد.

Shirin Razavian

Grapes of Happiness

Juicier than grapes on the vine
are these grapes of happiness.
Bright with dew from the heart,
I am a child once more.

Hope shoots green
in every corner
and silken strands of moonlight
slip through cracks in the window frame.

I have cut war's cruel buds
before they can blossom
and have tossed deep into a ravine
the phial that held my tears
and the life of the demon of sorrow.

I have split the body of darkness –
and its blood was white
and a part of the page of life.

I have entered poverty and hunger
on the list of diseases
soon to be cured.

Bread can kill hunger;
poverty need not prevent happiness.

One day
                I will cure all pain.

Translated from Farsi by Robert Chandler.

‖ *Iraq* ‖

Siduri Uruk

مواصفات العريس اللي تتمناه كل عروسة عراقية

آني بنت عراقية
صبية جميلة
حلوة ؟ أكيد حلوة
لأن ماكو عراقية ما تملي العين
أحلم مثل كل البنات
لا مو مثل كل البنات لأن آني عراقية
والعراقية ما تشبه أي البنات
أحلم بعريس زين يحمل هواية صفات
هي صفات بسيطة
بس كلش مهمة إلي كعراقية
باختصار آني عروس إلها شروط ومتطلبات
وأعتقد أنو مو هواية عليه
لأن آني عراقية
أحلم بعريس يحبني أكثر من كل البنات
وأكثر حتى من حوريات السماوات
أحلم بعريس مثقف أنيق
مو لابس بجامة ونعال ومتطوع بالمليشيات
أحلم بعريس ما ينتمي لأي حزب أو هيئة أو تيار
أريده ينتمي بس لأرض العراق
أحلم بعريس مدرس، مهندس، عامل
بس ما أريده بعد دكتور
أحلم بأديب، شاعر، كاتب
بس لا يكتب عن الديمقراطية والإنتخابات
ولا يكتب قصايد عن الأحزاب والفدرالية
أريد بيت على شواطىء الأعظمية
والذهب من سوق الكاظمية
أريد بحنة البصرة أنقش إيديه
وبخلاخل الموصل أزين رجليه

أريد عريس أهله من المذهبين

أريد بعرسي تدبك فرقة العلم

ويغني ماجد المهندس

وبعد أحسن لو وياهم لندا جورج شحرورة الكلدوآشوريين

أريد عريس يلبس بالعرس قاط وأحلى رباط

ولا يكلي الرباط مو عادتنا

لأن آني عروسة عراقية مو فارسية

يلبس دشداشة همينة ميخالف

بس لا يكصرها عبالك ده ينافس صبايا لبنان

لأن آني عروسة عراقية مو سعودية

أريد آني البس فستان أبيض جميل

وأنثر شعري الطويل

ولا يكلي شنو هاي؟

لأن آني عروسة عراقية مو أفغانية

أريد عرسي يكون عرس عراقي مغنى وهلاهل وفرح

ولا يزعل الجنسين

أريد شهر عسل بجبال السليمانية

بس لا يفرشولي سجادة حمرة

ويستقبلوني بحرس وفرقة وإستعراض

لأن آني مثلهم عراقية

أقصد همه مثلنا عراقيين

أتمنى الله يرزقني بأولاد وبنات حلويين

من يسألوني : يمه أحنا كلدانيين لو آشوريين

أهم على حلكهم وأكوللهم:

أنجبوا انتو عراقيين وبس

العفو، نسيت... إحنا ببلد ديمقراطي

العنف وال ضد القوانين

راح أحضنهم بحب وحنان وأكوللهم

أكسكيوزمي ماي جلدرن

إنتو عراقيين وبس... وهذا هو المهم

وصدكوني هذا حلم كل بنت عراقية

Siduri Uruk

An Iraqi Girl's Dream of a Bridegroom*

I am an Iraqi girl,
A beautiful Baghdad lass
Nice? Of course, nice
Because there is no Iraqi girl who doesn't appeal to the heart and to the eye
I dream like all the girls
No, not quite like all the girls, because I am an Iraqi girl
And the Iraqi girl doesn't resemble just any girls
I dream of a good bridegroom, who has many attributes,
That are simple attributes
But they are very important to me as an Iraqi girl
In brief, I am a bride, who has requirements and conditions
And I believe I am not asking for too much
Because I am an Iraqi girl
I dream of a bridegroom who loves me more than all the girls
And even more than the nymphs high up in the skies
I dream of a handsome, cultured bridegroom,
Not wearing pyjamas and flip flops and a volunteer in the militias
I dream of a bridegroom not affiliated to any party,
    committee or grouping
I want him to belong only to Iraq's soil
I dream of a bridegroom as a teacher, an engineer or a labourer
But I don't any more want him with a doctorate
I dream of a man of letters, a poet, a writer
But not one who writes on democracy and elections,
Nor one who pens poems to parties and federalism
I want a home down by the riverside in Al-A'dhemiye
And the gold from up the market in Al-Kadhimiye
I want to manicure my hands with henna from Al-Basra
I want to decorate my legs with anklets from Al-Mosul
I want a bridegroom whose parents come from both sects
Whose friends are Kurds, and whose neighbours are Christians
Together with Sabeans and Turcoman
At my wedding, I want the Al-'Alam band** to play the music
And the good old Hatem Al-Asmer to sing

Better still, if accompanied by Linda George, the nightingale
    of Chaldo-Assyrians
I want a bridegroom dressed at the wedding in a suit and the nicest tie
And who doesn't tell me that wearing the tie isn't our custom
Because, I am an Iraqi bride, not a Persian one
If he wears a dishdashe gown,*** it still doesn't matter
Provided he doesn't shorten it as if he is competing with
    Lebanon's young girls
Because I am an Iraqi bride, not a Saudi one
I want to wear a beautiful white dress and loosen my long hair
And he doesn't tell me that it is taboo, or that I should wear the veil
Because I am an Iraqi bride, not an Afghan one
I want my wedding to be an Iraqi wedding with merriment,
    singsongs and ululations
And that doesn't segregate the two sexes and say it is an
    Islamic wedding and celebration
Because I am an Iraqi bride, not a Jordanian Bedouin one
I want a honeymoon in the mountains of Dihouk and Al-Suleymaniye
Provided they don't lay a red carpet with the reception
By a guard of honour and marching with a band
Because, like them, I am an Iraqi
I mean, like us, they are Iraqis
I wish for God to bless me with nice boys and girls
When they ask me: Mum! Are we Sunni or Shi'a?
I will smack their gobs and tell them:
Shut up! You are Iraqis, full stop.
I beg your pardon! I forgot we are in a democratic country
Violence and beatings are against the law
I will embrace them lovingly and affectionately and tell them:
Excuse me, my children****
You are Iraqis and nothing else and this is what is important
And believe you me! This is the dream of every Iraqi girl.

Translated from colloquial Iraqi Arabic by M. T. Ali.
*The title of the poem in Arabic is "The Personnel Specifications of a Bride-groom as the Wishes of Every Iraqi Bride."
**Al-'Alam, which means the flag, is the name of a music band from Salah-Al-Deen county.
***A *dishdashe* is the traditional loose, flowing gown worn by Arab men.
****"Excuse me, my children" was originally in English.

Saadi Youssef

سعادة

مل ء عينيك
ثم شجيرات ورد
وأغصان ليمونة...
....
....
....
وبيوت الحجر
—البيوت التي تكره—
تصعد أعلى فأعلى
مبللة بالمطر.
ليس يكفي التأمل...
ما أسعد المرء يفتح نافذة
في الصباح!

Saadi Youssef

Happiness

To fill your eyes
there are rose shrubs
and branches of a lemon tree.

The stone houses
you once hated
rise higher and higher
wet with rain.

Thinking is not enough.

O
happy is a man
who opens a window
unto the morning!

Translated from Arabic by Khaled Mattawa.

‖ Japan ‖

Mimi Hachikai

あなたとわたし

長い時間がたったのだろう
忘れていた道を
ふたたびたどり
曲がり角を折れる
あのころと変わらない森が
いまも息をしている
一枚また一枚　葉を手放しながら
日々のページをめくる森
季節の本はぶあつくて
いつも読みきれない
「ここにいるよ」
合図をすると
ふりむくのはあなた
新緑と紅葉のあいだから
若葉と落ち葉のあいだから
こちらを見る
瞬間、
目が合う
それは遠い日
いつのまにか過ぎ去った日
森のあいだからビルが生えて
霧は消え　泉がかれて
やわらかな土が沈黙しても
おぼえている　きっと
見えなくなっても
おぼえている
そこにいたことを
だから、
いつでも
わたしたちはそこにいる

Mimi Hachikai

You and I

It feels like a long time.
I am now again following the way
That I almost forgot.
Turning the corner,
There I find the same forest
Breathing, just like those days.
Leaf after leaf it lets go,
Page after page it turns over each day.
So thick is a season's book,
Impossible to read it all.
"I am here."
When I wave,
You turn to me
And look at me
Between tender green and autumn color,
Between young leaves and fallen leaves.
Our gazes meet
Just for a fleeting second.
It was so long ago.
Amidst forest trees buildings may have grown,
Mists, vanished, and springs, dried up.
Still, I shall surely remember you.
Still, I shall surely remember
That we were here.

Translated from Japanese by Harashita Sunaoshi.

Amira El-Zein

Lightness

In translucent grapes
we sit
and chant
"Master of the horizon,
our distant father,
O Palm of Light!"

Between two dawns
we descend
with our grandmothers,
spinning skeins of morning.

We enter the dreams
of the living,
dust-free,
water filling our mouths,
and sand rolling up
under our heels,
while we sway
from chest
to waist,
in basket-rings,
in a sphere-shaped house,
we penetrate thick forests
of love, chanting:
"O Master of the Horizon!
Grant our hearts
the food of Eternity!"

Joumana Haddad

Plato's Song

Philosophers say it's impossible;
Cynics consider it naïve;

And yet
there it is:

A smile on the face of a total stranger
whom you'll probably never meet again.

The giggle of a baby
reminding you
of the first time your mother called your name.

A bird that suddenly lands on your balcony,
sings a gentle song,
then flies away
leaving a scent of freedom behind.

The sounds of the world just before dawn,
uncorrupted,
effortless,
as easy as life appears to be
from the warmth of a womb:
The fingerprints of what was,
the hopes of what could be.

Your heart bursting with love,
nothing
but
pure
love.

An unexpected kiss
on your bleeding wound,
and the knife in your aching back
whispering: "Keep going! Keep going!"

The hug at goodbye,
the hug at hello again,
and the longing in between.

Walking barefoot on a quiet beach,
then sitting down in a busy street
picturing the moment that each passer-by
has said "I love you"
and meant it.

Recognizing an old friend
in the eyes of a child
in a foreign city
where handmade necklaces are sold for a nickel,
and serenity is given away.

Breaking free from what you've been told to think,
to believe
to say
to do;
Breaking free from what you've been told to be.

Leaving behind what has to be left,
shedding your skin to find a new you.

The thought that you can,
the thrill that you might,
the certainty that you will.

Being grateful to a plant,
a humble plant
that is there just to let you breathe,
not expecting anything in return.

Finding peace
despite the terror
the doubts
the misunderstandings
the pain that's trying to eat you up
like a fire in a burning building
with no emergency exits.

The gift of the right words
said at the right time.

Inventing what ought to be invented,
accepting what you cannot change
just yet.

Coffee.
Yes, simply coffee,
and new clothes
and those nice leather shoes you wore
to your best friend's wedding;
thanking the little hands in the factory
or on the fields
that made all of this possible for you.

Bread.
The smell of bread,
and then, vaccines,
of course,
and cures for cancer,
and those who are bent over their microscopes all day
trying to keep you safe,
and those who are cleaning the roads
while you are asleep -
but whose names will forever be unknown to you.

The immensity of the universe,
the happy coincidence of you being in it;
All the atoms and unlikely series of events
that have allowed you to happen
against all odds.

The mistakes you made,
the lessons you learned
and the dreams you tell no one about.

Your body;
The magnificence of it:
A perfect machine at your service.

Your mind
and all you can do with it,
which will always be more than you will ever know.

The beauty of poets who doubt themselves,
The beauty of scientists
who never do.

Saying no despite the fear,
saying yes without regrets.

Realizing you are not lonely;
Realizing you are not alone,
and that the "other" they taught you to hate so much
is a mere refraction of who you are:
One of your endless possibilities.

Giving,
constantly;
Giving even what you think you do not have
(Oh, but sure you do!).

Playing like a kid,
like a grownup who saved that kid inside
from drowning.

Bees, ants, butterflies,
and all the tiny creatures
who lead a quiet existence
unaware of what a Sunday brunch is;
Not needing the Ferrari
that their neighbor has bought
in order to feel fulfilled.

The insignificance of you,
the majesty of you,
and forgetting both
while looking at a star
that is looking at you too...

◆ ◆ ◆

Philosophers say it's naïve;
Cynics consider it impossible;

And yet
here it is:

Easier than what you've been told,
closer than you imagine:
A magical tree
in a child's fairy tale
patiently
waiting
for your human embrace.

|| *Malaysia* ||

Shirley Lim

When

When I was a child, I would watch the spray
Break phosphorescence at my feet then run away.
There was so much sea, always rhythmically
And gently pulling to the horizon.
There was the enormous starry clarity
Of sky and sharply carried upon
The breeze the smells of pines and salty sea.
It was a child's preoccupation
To stare at the yellow coin of moon,
To crumble pine needles between thumb and finger,
Not thinking anything particular, to linger,
Watching the trees bend in the wind, sea dance,
Till you knew it was time to be home soon,
And straightaway left with no backward glance.

|| *Nepal* ||

Thakur Prasad Mainali

परमानन्द

कामको गोहीलाई अहिंसाको हतियारले टुक्रयाइदेऊ
क्रोधको डढेलोलाई दयाको वर्षाले निभाईदेऊ ।
लोभको भूमरीमा सुकेको पात भैँ घुमिरहेको मलाई
आमाको काखजस्तो शरण दिएर बचाई देऊ प्रभु !

अबोध बालक जस्तै म आफ्नै अहंमा हिँडिरहेछु
म आफ्नै डाहको डढेलोमा पिल्सिइरहेछु
यसैले मलाई कुकर्मबाट बचाई आनन्द देऊ
अविश्वास र असमानताको शत्रुबाट मुक्त गराईदेऊ प्रभु !

आशक्ति रीस राग र मोहको जालबाट मुक्त बनाऊ
आत्मविश्वास र शान्तिको उज्यालोतिर डोर्‍याऊ
अभिमान र निष्ठुरताले ग्रस्त भएको बेला
दया र करुणाका दुवै हात फिजाएर साथ लेऊ प्रभु !

आरतीको प्रकाशजस्तै मेरो मन उज्यालो पार्न सकूँ
सूर्य र चन्द्रमाको किरण जस्तै तिमीसँगै फैलिन सकूँ
मान-अपमान, सुख-दुःख आदिमा समान बन्न सकूँ
त्याग, तपस्या र समानताको बाटोमा हिँड्न सकूँ प्रभू !

Thakur Prasad Mainali

Supreme Bliss

Destroy the desire-crocodile with a weapon of non-violence,
Put out the wild fire of anger with the shower of compassion
I am being blown like a dry leaf in the whirlpool of greed
My Lord! Save this soul like an infant on its mother's lap,
 O God, give me refuge at Your Feet and protect me.

Like a sulking child I am walking in my own pride
I am being scorched in the wildfire of my own jealousy
Therefore save me from my committing wrong deeds
Liberate me, my Lord, from the hands of my enemies –
    faithlessness.

Free me from the bondage of anger and attachment,
Lead me towards the light of peace and self-confidence
From depths of ego and ruthlessness take me out
Stretch your compassionate and benevolent Hands O God
And hold me tight!

Like the lamp offered to God, may my heart be full of Light
Like the sun rays and moon beams let me radiate in You,
    O God
In praise, insults, happiness and sorrow let me remain in
    equanimity
Let me traverse along the paths of dedication, devotion, and
    equality, my Lord.

Translated from Nepalese by Govinda Raj Bhattarai.

Shazea Quraishi

My Mother's Embroidered Apron

I am lost in my mother's apron –
green parrots drip from the trees,
a peacock brushes past me
pulling its clockwork tail of children's dreams.
I breathe in the heat of cinnamon,
the fug of yeast. My mother's voice
fills me like smoke and her stories
lift me – I rise like a yellow balloon,
my feet, white ribbons trailing in the long, wet grass.

Jim Pascual Agustin

Puddles after the First Monsoon Rain

The secret breath of summer
curls from his lips, blurs
the gray, melting world
on the other side of the glass.

Early monsoon runs
lightly on tin roofs,
then swiftly retreats
to the greens of distant hills.

Doors along the narrow line
of houses burst open with children
even as banana leaves bend to drop
the last beads of rain down their palms.

He is among them, this boy
with the breath of summer.
The palpable scent of earth
roused by rain, fills his lungs.

He runs in zigzags to his friends,
making sure to hit every puddle
with every leap. The louder
the splash, the better.

Mud must be spread far and wide.
The undeclared ritual
to celebrate the slightest change
of tropical seasons.

Marjorie Evasco

Huni sa Kawhaa'g Tulo Ka Adlaw Sa Ulan

Nagtulo ang atup, nagkalingaw pa'g ulan.
Ang akong mga kaldero'g kulon napuno'g katunga
Sa mga huni sa ting-habagat.

Third World Music on the 23rd Day of Rain

Roof leaks, still falls rain.
My pots and pans fill, half-full
With monsoon music.

Translated from English to Cebuano-Binisaya by Marjorie Evasco.

Victor Peñaranda

Morning Walk
Mongar, Bhutan

Morning approaches, bare and golden,
Whispering, seductive as fallen light
On moss, touching without forgetting . . .
I'm woven into silence in this wilderness
Where birdsong is released from the leaf
By a vow of the ephemeral . . .
Slowly, the universe emerges from sleep
Knowing the moment when all is God . . .
Somewhere, a tree clings gently to the breeze.

‖ *Republic of Korea* ‖

Ko Un

행복이여 호젓하여라

누가 알랴
시베리아에서 오세아니아까지
몇날며칠 밤으로 낮으로
한 떼거리 철새들 절망 없이 하늘 건너간다

누가 알랴
저 유라시아 서녘에서
동아시아까지
동아시아 지나
알류산열도 밑 북태평양까지
자전(自轉)의 행성 편서풍(偏西風) 쉬지 않고 건너간다

누가 알랴
세상의 바다 해류 조류 무릅쓰고
몇 년 뒤의 먼 고향
한 생애를 바치는 늙은 연어떼들 물속으로 건너간다

누가 알랴
한반도 한 뙈기 밭두렁
해 뜨고 해 지는 내내
밭 일손 놓지 않고 등 굽은 늙은 남정네의 삶이
눈먼 세월을 건너간다

누가 알랴
저 건너 산 그림자
그 산 그림자 건너
여기 저문 해 남아있는 비탈
호미 놓고 아기 젖 먹이는 엄마의 사랑은 산야를 건너간다

누가 알랴
누가 알랴

Ko Un

Be Indistinct, Happiness

Who would know?
Flocks of migrant birds fly across the sky with no despair
by day by night,
from Siberia to Oceania.

Who would know?
The revolving planet's westerly winds blow past with no
rest
from the western part of Eurasia
to East Asia,
beyond East Asia
to the North Pacific below the Aleutian Islands.

Who would know?
Shoals of old salmon swim across the water
braving the ocean tides and currents,
devoting their lives
to the far-away home they left years before.

Who would know?
The life of a bent old man passes through blind time
as he works
on a scrap of paddy field in the Korean peninsula
from sunrise to sunset.

Who would know?
The love of a mother passes over the hills and fields
as she lays down her hoe and breastfeeds her baby
here on a slope where the sun still shines
opposite the mountain shadow over there.

Who would know?
Who would know?

Translated from Korean by Lee Sang-Wha and Brother Anthony.

|| *Sri Lanka* ||

Mary Anne Mohanraj

Learning the Hour

I am learning the hour of three a.m.
the chill in the living room
until I start the gas fire hissing
dark pressing down on my eyelids.
Wrapped in a cream blanket
so tired, but restless, unable to sleep
she hasn't slept for hours
with the ache in her jaw
small, sharp pains stabbing up
hurling her from sleep to whimper
then howl, in the cage of white wood slats.
He takes her from her crib over and over
soothes her back to sleep
but only resting against the warmth
of a body can she drift deeper,
beyond the reach of the small, new bone,
cutting through tender flesh. At three a.m.
I take pity on him. Climb out of bed
say go to sleep — I'll take her
the living burden shifts from arms
to arms. I carry her carefully
down the wooden stairs; we settle on the couch
to whispered shushings, songs of sleep
fingers grazing the softness of her cheek.

|| *State of Palestine* ||

Maya Abu Al-Hayat

مسافة

سأهديك أرضا

من تحت الأذن

حتى حافة الكتف اليسرى

هناك أزرع الفقوس

والفراولة والعنب

لا تحصد شيئا

فقط أزرع لتنمو الأشياء

وقبل أن ترخي الأغصان بحماوتها على الأرض

قبل أن تنفجر الثمار وتصرخ

(كلوني)

قبل أن يحين للأخضر أن يصبح رمادا

فقط تلك اللحظة

أحصد شيئا من الفراولة

وازرعها في قلبي

Maya Abu Al-Hayat

Distance

My gift to you
will be a land
stretching from the end of the left ear
to the border of the left shoulder
where I plant cucumber, strawberry, grapes
and you won't have to worry
about harvest
I'll simply plant
so that trees may grow
and just before their branches drop
their feverish load to the ground
just before the fruits explode
and scream "eat me"
just before what's green turns to ash
I'll return
to pick some strawberries
and plant them in my heart
to turn my heart red

Translated from Arabic by Fady Joudah.

Adonis

غداً

متى أرى : لي مشرقٌ جامحٌ
يبتكر الشمس ، ولي مغربُ
متى أرى، والكون لي ملعبُ
والحبّ والعزّة لي ساعدانْ ؛
قلبيَ للثّورة مستنفَرٌ
. دقّاته صارت زمانَ الزّمانْ

Adonis

Tomorrow

When will I see
that I have an untamable east
that invents the sun,
and I that have a west,
and wherever I look
the world is my field of play,
love and pride my very arms.
My heart stands taut with rebellion,
its pulse keeps time for time.

Translated from Arabic by Khaled Mattawa.

Guzal Begim

Счастье цвета фиалки

Чучмома нафасин сезиб уйғондим
икки кўзим орасига қўшиқлар тўккан
сен ям-яшил туғёнсан баҳор

Қушлар овозимни тонгда талашди
китоб ўқиб берсам сукунатга мен
дарахтлар чайқалди қадийм оҳангда

Қалдирғоч қаноти қошимга тегиб
кўкламдан кўкламга қувилганимда
майсалар қонида туғилдим қайта

Қўлимдан ушлади шабнимнинг бўйи
таралиб турди-да мутаносиб куй
бинафша рўйи ўй сурди руҳимда

Бўш қолмади биронта бўшлиқ
нилуфар тасаввурин ҳадя қил баҳор
юрагимда тонг оттирсин сабо

Guzal Begim

Happiness in the Color of Violet

I awoke to the breath of crocus
a flood of song struck me right between the eyes
you bright-green riot spring

The birds set to squabbling over my voice at dawn
as I read a book aloud to the silence
trees swaying to the ancient song

When the swallow's wing touched my brow
I was cast out of one spring into another
reborn in the veins of new leaves

The fragrance of dew seized me by the hand
its music scattered in all directions
the color of violets sat meditating in my soul

No single empty space remains empty
grant me the lily's imagination, spring
let the morning breeze keep vigil in my heart

Translated from Uzbek by Rachel Harrell.

EUROPE

Photo: Unmesh Swanson

|| *Bulgaria* ||

Tsvetanka Elenkova

ЧЕРНИ ВРЪХ

На върха. Само една тревичка между мен и небето. Навсякъде теменужки. Земята - влажна и топла, загряваш компрес, обичащо тяло. Лекува ме цяла. Навсякъде камъни. Като в индианско типи преди свещения ритуал на лулите. Камъни, по-големи от реките, без те да са пресъхнали. Сурова красота, не благородна, да си счупиш кътник. Но и благородна, заради водата. Колко е хубаво, когато някой бие камбаната, когато всеки бие камбаната – не на църквата, на метеорологичната станция. 2290 метра по-близо до Бог.

Cherni Vrah

At the summit. Just a little grass between me and heaven. Violets everywhere. The earth wet and warm, a hot compress, a loving body. It heals me all over. Stones everywhere. As in an Indian tepee before the sacred ritual of the pipe. Stones bigger than the rivers, even though they're not dry. An austere, not gentle beauty – you'll break a tooth. But gentle as well, because of the water. How lovely it is when someone rings the bell, when everyone rings the bell – not of the church but of the meteorological station – 2290 metres closer to God.

Translated from Bulgarian by Jonathan Dunne.

|| *Finland* ||

Ilpo Tiihonen

Kesäillan kevyt käsitteellisyys

Oi kesäiltaa, sen illallisuutta
oi sen ihmeiden ilmeistä sillallisuutta
kun yöhön yhtyy sen laineettomuus
ja ryhtyy ihmiseen paineettomuus

Oi lehmisyyttä ja ihmisyyttä,
oi värjyvän väreilevyyttä,
viatonten vaarattomuutta
ja laajuuden levollisuutta –
uikun poikasta, viittä kuutta
ja syvää vettä, sylillisyyttä.

Oi peilitaivaamme sinisen siirtyvyys
ja kuusten latvallisuus, pyhä piirtyvyys,
ja mustan laulajan huiluilevuus.
Sisäkkäisyys, muiluilevuus!

Ja oi joutilaan joutavaa joutavaisuutta
ja oi soutajan sukkulaa soutavaisuutta
lomamatkalla määrättömyyteen
ja oi rannalla onkijan pyyteettömyys,
solvaukseton syyteettömyys,
kun pää on päätynyt jäärättömyyteen.

Suven suuruus, suvi suvi, sen kaikuilevuutta,
saunasauhujen haikuilevuutta, lip lap
laiturillisuus lip, lap kiikuttavuus
ja ihon alaston liikuttavuus
ja korkea kaikujen lokillisuus
ja pihapiirien kokillisuus.

Ilpo Tiihonen

A summer evening's
slight conceptualness

Ah summer evening, and its eveningness,
its prodigious wonders and their bridgefulness
when the night-united seamlessness
steals into one's heart with restfulness

O heiferiness and humanness,
ah shivering shimmeringness,
innocents' innocuousness
and vastness with its stresslessness –
five or six chicks of a dabchick,
and deep water, lapfulness.

Our blue sky's mirrored changefulness!
the spruces' tall topliness, their tips' sacredness
the yellow-billed black singer's flutiness.
Nested cosiness, mutual tootiness!

And oh the idler's idling idleness
and the shuttling rower's glidingness
on his holiday trip to goal-lessness
the fisherman's undemanding uncatchingness
the innocent non-offendingness
of the leadhead's letting-go-ingness.

Summer, great echoing summer's heatstrokiness,
the haiku-puffs of the sauna's smokiness, lip-lap
unsteady jettiness, lip-lap, rocking-about-edness
the naked skin's nothing-about-it-edness
aerial echoing of seagullness
and goodies grilling for forkedness.

Oi salmisuus, ulappuus, virrallisuus
Oi höyhenenkeveä irrallisuus
ja maan seisminen staatillisuus

ja kesätyvenen paatillisuus.

Oi lehmisyys, ihmisyys, levollisuus,
oi suomenhevosten suopea hevollisuus,
ketunpoikien raikuli revollisuus,
pyiden pyisyys ja kyiden kyisyys,
oi vielä kaukana syys, tyly yisyys!

Oi mikroskooppinen multava matous,
voikukkien aurinkosatous,
pientarillinen heinyys, sen huojahtavuus
ja juolaheinien mieleenjuolahtavuus
ja suolaheinien suloinen suolaisuus!

Oi kaikki rakkaiden kielellä kuolaisuus
kuin lemmenvuokkojen tuoksujen vuolaisuus
ja mesiheinien huumaava kiimallisuus
Ja huulikukkasten melkeinpä liimallisuus

niin, ja onnen laidalla ohdakkeisuus.
Vaan kohta kohdalta kaikkeuden kohdakkeisuus
ja viite viitteeltä vihreä viitteellisyys
soi ihmislaulujen liitteellisyys!
Oi kaikki lehmisyys, ihmisyys, leijallisuus
ja pilvikorkeus, korkeuden laulullisuus
kuin taivashuoneemme huoneentaulullisuus,
oi kesän heijallerii, kaikki heijallisuus!

Ah gulfiness, lakiness, streaminess
ah featherlight set-free-again-ness
and seismic earth's ecstatic staticness

and summer calm's so easy boatliness.

Ah cows' exuberant udderliness,
humanness, quiescentness,
ah Finnish horses' trusty horsiness,
and foxcubs' frisky foxiness,

hazelhens' henness, snakes' snakiness,
ah far-off-ness of quaky autumn, and its headachiness!

Oh microscopic wormy mouldiness
dandelions' sunny harvest of goldiness
the headland's swaying hayfulness
witchgrass's whimsical playfulness
and sheep-sorrel's sweet salt-tastiness!
Oh the saliva-licking of all unchasteness
hot musk-orchid's scented headiness
passion flowers' glad gift of unsteadiness
and the minty gluiness of sticky lipfulness

yes, and at the edge of happiness, thistliness.
But detail by detail the cosmic interdependenceness
and ref by ref its green inter-referenceness
sing the appendixness of human songfulness
Oh all the heiferiness, humanness, hoveringness
wafting cloud-loftiness, lofty melodiousness –
our heavenly household's wall-hung wise-sayingness –
oh summer cradling us, its total cradlingness.

Translated from Finnish by Herbert Lomas (assisted by Soila Lehtonen).

|| *France* ||

Pascale Petit

Blue-and-Gold
Macaw Feather

Just a feather on the aviary floor –
I hold it to the light. Sapphire
one side of the shaft, lapis

on the other, like earth's arc
as it tilts into space.

And the underside, sulphur
as a field of rape,* is a palette
where cadmiums roil.

I balance the fallen blade
between thumb and forefinger.

I could paint a world
with this brush, these hues.

Is this how God felt as He drew
His colours across the void?

---

*Rape, a yellow-flowered plant of the mustard family native to Europe.

|| *Georgia* ||

Dato Barbakadze

ცუდი ამინდის შემდეგ

მართაია წვიმა ნაავიდა, მაგრამ რადაცა მაინც დატოვა
გაცრუებული იმედების, სვეტი ხეების, დახურული წიგნების სახით;
რადაც, აღბათ, დამთავრდა კიდეც, მაგრამ ცხოვრება გრძელდება,
ცხოვრება გრძელდება წარსულისაკენ,
რომეიც კიდევ ბევრ ძვირფას შეხებას გაიყოლებს,
ერთმანეთით ამოავსებს ნივთებს შორის ცვაღებაღ მანძილს,
ერთმანეთში ჩაანაცვლებს სუე სხვაღასხვა მიმართულებით აჩქარებუღ
გამოცდიღებებს,
ყოვეღთვის იმოძრავებს გზა, რომეღმაც ერთმანეთს უნდა შეახვეღროს
აღამიანები და სიმღერები,
ღექსები და ფრინვეღები,
თვაღი და ღანა;
ის კი, ერთი ურიცხვთაგანი, რაღაცას ეძებს,
რაღაც ისეთს, რასაც ერთ ღროს ერთად ვექებდით,
რაც ვერ წარხოცეს შენეღებეუღმა ღამემ და მშვიღობამ,
რაც მოინეეა მრავაღმა სოციაღურმა კუჭმა,
რაც ღამთავრღა,
მაგრამ აი, ღროს კი, იმ ჩვენს ღროს,
ჩვენს მოპოვებუე ანწყოს ღა წვაღებას, ვერ გამოვტაცეთ;
ვერ გამოვტაცეთ ვერც სვეე ხეებს,
ვერც ჩვენს სამშობეოს,
რომეიც ნეღ-ნეღა ემსგავსება ისეთ თავის თავს,
სატრფოს რომ ვეღარ შევაღარებთ;
ვერ გამოვტაცეთ ჩვენს სურვიღს -
ცოტა უფრო ღიღხანს რქმეოდა სიყვარუღი იმას,
რაც შემთხვევის წყაღობით მოგვეეა.
მაგრამ, როგორც ჩანს, სადღაც მაინც ხარ,
თუნღაც ერთი ურიცხვთაგანი,
რაღაცით ღაღიღი, რაღაცის მოიმეღე,
სიკეთის ღოკაღური გამოვღინებისთვის მაღღობის გაღამხღეღი;

ყოველთვის იმოძრავებს გზა, რომელიც ზოგჯერ კივიდით ჩაიქროდებს,
ზოგჯერ მთელი წლით, საუკუნით ან წამის მთელი მეათასედით დაგვიანდება,
ზოგჯერ - რატომდაც - მაშინ მოვა, როცა სხვაგან ვართ,
მაგრამ წვიმამ ხომ ჩვენი სახით რადაც ისეთი შეატოვა
სვეე ხეებს და სვეე მოაჯირებს,
რაც, აღათ, დიღხანს უნდა განვაღდეს,
წარსუღიღან მოსატაცებღად კიღევ დიღხანს არ გაიმეტოს
ის, რაც მართაღა იყო,
რამაც სასტიკი ხეღი გვკრა და არაერთი გუღივით დაგვწყდა,
რათა ერთად და ერთმანეთისთვის გაღავერჩინეთ,
რათა დავკარგვოღით ნივთებს შორის მონიშნუღ მანძილს,
ყოველთვის ცვაღებაღს, ყოველთვის მარტივს.

Dato Barbakadze

After Bad Weather

It's true the rain left, but when it left, it left something behind
in the form of unfulfilled hopes, wet trees, closed books –
something probably ended as well. But life goes on,
life keeps heading toward the past,
which will still take with it many a precious touch,
will fill the changing distance between objects with the objects themselves,
will replace experiences hurrying in opposite directions with each other;
the road always moves, which should lead to the meeting of people and songs,
poetry and guineafowl
the eye and the knife
and he, one of the innumerable, is seeking something,
something we once sought together
that wasn't erased by slowing nights and peace,
that was ruminated on by many a social stomach
and ended.
But still, from that time, from our time,
the present and the trouble, we couldn't tear it away,
couldn't wrest it from the wet trees
nor from our country,
which step by step begins to resemble itself again,
so we can't compare her to our beloved any more.
We couldn't wrest it from our desire –
to be allowed a little longer to call
that which was given to us accidentally love,
But you still seem to be somewhere,

even when you are one of the innumerable,
tired of one thing, hoping for another,
grateful for any local displays of kindness.
The road will always move, will sometimes be swept by screams,
will be delayed for a whole year, a century, one whole thousandth
of a second.
Sometimes, somehow, for unknown reasons, it will come when
    we aren't there,
but the rain somehow left something behind
for wet trees and slippery railings,
which should probably be troubled for a long time
because a long time will keep
what really was from being kidnapped,
that which pushed us away with cruel hand and broke us like
hearts,
did so to save us both, together, for each other,
lost to the marked distance
between objects
always changing, always simple.

*Translated from Georgian by Lyn Coffin with the assistance
of Nato Alhazishvili.*

Gernot Blume

Sterntaler

Die Suche nach Glück
braucht günstige Beleuchtung,
damit sie kurze Schatten wirft.

Light

The search for happiness
needs favorable lighting
to cast short shadows.

Translated from German by Gernot Blume.

‖ *Hungary* ‖

George Szirtes

We Love Life Whenever We Can

For Mimi Khalvati, after Mahmoud Darwish

We love life whenever we can.
We enter the grocer's, the baker's, the chemist's
 the post office daily.
We love life whenever we can.
We borrow each other's books and paperclips
 and forget to return them.
We spruce ourselves up for a meeting, order
 a taxi, climb into a bus or a train.
We love life whenever we can
 and so we sign letters and cards and spend
 the evening walking the street
When the winter is fiercest and the light
 in the windows and amusement arcades
 snarls at the darkness and the sea is quietly chomping at
 the cliff and the owl and the rat and the fox move over
and
 through and we hear them and listen.
We love life whenever we can.

|| *Ireland* ||

Peter Fallon

Day and Night

Day – the great adventure
still in store. Time
and time again, one foot
before the other, I climb

among the foothills
that become a life.
We've children now
and I, like my good wife,

must learn the art
of letting go.
For, as Leonardo knew, only

Breda Wall Ryan

Discoveries

Moulded to your father's shoulders and neck,
you ride home from the beach, his fingers
braceleting ankles and wrists.
Your head in the palm of his hand, an acorn
snug in its cup. You, curled
to your mother's breast; a puzzle, complete.

In time you learned the world, my girl, blissed
in your golden spheres and swirls, that time
of waking every day to the new,
the bicycle *whing* of going-home swans,
your first cold taste of sky-falling snow,
the snail's horns pulled from your kiss, gone;

the wind made of sand; the sea
was washing its weeds.

Now the girl riding your father's back is yours.
She stands on his stirrup-hips, fingers
clasping his ears — reins!
They canter through woods to the strand, crouch
head-to-head by a rockpool.
And you — *click!* The picture, complete.

She's learning the world, your girl, amazed
at the everyday new; a pretty blue flame, hot!
The growl of a coming-on storm,
raindrops smash where they fall,
tiny winkles and stones in a jar, huge!
The snail comes to her song. A tickled anemone, gone!

And the wind's made of sand, the sea
is still washing its weeds.

‖ *Israel* ‖

Rosebud Ben-Oni

הָאֹמֵר

לחיים, לדרכים החדשות
שתגלי, לצבע רענן ולח,
ורגבים חדשים
שאחרי רעידת האדמה,
נוחי ועברי את המדבריות, מרדי
כנגד הזרקורים,
גמעי את זעקות הים הגועשים
והאזיני לשירים עבורך
מצאי העומקים הנצחיים חשוכי המרפא ודעי
שלא תוכלי לנקות את חדרך
בהסתתרות מתחת למיטה.
לשאלות, **למדוע**
ואז **מדוע** שוב
כאריה, לבקרים
הנוהמים כקלידי אורגן ממורקים,
לעכבישים במקלחות קיץ,
לאהבה כנה כמטבעות שנמצאו בטלפון ציבורי,
לנרות אחרונים, לאהבה ראשונה, ערפל
ותחרה, תמצאי את דרכך,
חרטי ספרות רומיות בעצים
ותמצאי נשים חכמות תחתיהן,
לשעותייך המאוחרות בערב, לספקנים שתפגשי,
שתהיי אפריל יותר מאביב, פרמי את תפרי
המשפטים, ודעי את הנצח,
דועך ואינסופי, כתר אור, בעת שאת שרה
את היום אל תוך הלילה.

Translated from English to Hebrew by Rosebud Ben-Oni.

Rosebud Ben-Oni

A Poem for My Niece
on No Particular Day

So here's to you, to the smudged, unsettled
paths you'll leave behind, to paint that never
dries, to new ground along old fault lines,
pause, and then–cross the blinding
dunes, defy the breach of a search
light, imbibe the screams of sea
clattering for you–
Know those incurable
depths, but know you cannot clean your room
by disappearing under the bed. So here's to asking
WHY–then WHY a second time
with the look of lion, to mornings that sound the burnished
pipes of an organ, to the daddy-long-legs over the summer
humming drains, to love as honest as spare change
found in a payphone, to last candles, to your first love, that fog
of the finest gossamer, may you find your way through it,
to Roman numerals a beloved carves into trees,
may you find the wise women beneath them,
to your late-in-the-evening, to skeptics you will meet,
may you be more April than Spring, may you unstitch the seams
of sentences, and from them know eternity,
ebbing and endless, crown of light, as you sing
the day–into night.

|| *Italy* ||

Alessandro De Francesco

stiamo sospesi sugli scalini

stiamo sospesi sugli scalini
sopra l'acqua
al centro c'è l'estate vista dall'alto
il buio della città
passa tra un fanale e l'altro

le superfici delle braccia aderiscono
e si rivelano lucide sotto
l'intermittenza di un'insegna

ogni poro è una distesa aperta
il corpo sogna i capelli
si dà nella forma del possibile

alcuni temerari nuotatori
si gettavano nelle acque della senna
risalivano la corrente
fino alla prima banchina

Alessandro De Francesco

we are suspended on the stairs

we are suspended on the stairs
above the water
in the center is the summer seen from above
the darkness of the city
passes from one headlight to the next

the surfaces of our arms cohere
and are shiny underneath
the blinking of a sign

each pore is an open expanse
the body dreams the hair
gives form to the possible

some daring swimmers
throw themselves into the Seine
they swim upstream
all the way until the first quay

Translated from Italian by Belle Cushing.

‖ *Luxembourg* ‖

Laurent Fels

au carrefour
de la

solitude
germe

parfois
la vie
à
l'ombre

at the

Translated from French by Jean-François Sené.

|| *Norway* ||

Marit Irene Jensen

Jeg Er En Stjerne

Jeg er en stjerne på livets himmel
Den mørkeste skygge lagt bak meg.

I Am A Star

I am a star in life's sky,
the darkest shadow left behind.

Translated from Norwegian by Marit Irene Jensen.

|| *Poland* ||

Zofia Beszczyńska

nagła chwila światła

nagła chwila światła
w ciemności
poruszenia wiatru w białym niebie

nad naszymi głowami anioły: ich
jaśniejące stopy
z drugiej strony tęczy

Zofia Beszczyńska

a sudden moment of light

a sudden moment of light
in the dark
movement of the wind in the white sky

over our heads the angels: their
glowing feet
on the other side of the rainbow

Translated from Polish by Agnieszka Kreczmar.

|| *Republic of Moldova* ||

Vika Chembartseva

ДИ-ЛИ-ДЖАН*, КОЛОКОЛЬЧИК ТУМАНА

Тишина.

Побледневшая ночь на террасе балкона.

Сквозь закрытые веки

разреженный воздух скользит золотистым свеченьем,

и плывут волоокие тёмные рыбы зрачков

и пугливою стайкой дрожат плавниками на радужке глаз.

И звучанье незримой реки –

колокольчик тумана, певучие горные воды -

Дилиджан, ди-ли-джан-ди-ли-джан-джан-джан-джан.

Это капля рассвета течёт по щеке,

розовея стыдливостью юного солнца.

Это птица зари, словно перья крыла, обронившая день.

Это ветер лениво качает свой хвойный предутренний веер.

Это рябь облаков

в прояснившейся сини клубится небесной отарой –

колокольчик тумана, певучие горные воды –

Дилиджан, ди-ли-джан-ди-ли-джан-джан-джан-джан.

Тишина…

Vika Chembartseva

Di-Li-Jan,* the Small Bell of Mist

Silence..
The night has turned pale on the terrace.
The rarefied air slides through closed eyes
    as a golden glow.
The pupils, a timid shoal of ox-eyed fishes,
        float and tremble like fins across the iris.
The sound of the river unseen.
The small bell of mist, the singing of the waters from
    the mountains.
Dilijan, di-li-jan-di-li-jan-jan-jan-jan!
That's the drop of sunrise flowing down your cheek
        modestly turning pink as the young sun rises.
That's the bird of dawn dropping
down the day as feathers on its wing.
That's the wind that lazily shakes the conifer's fan.
That's the ripple of cloud
        that coils like a herd across the deepening blue of
    the sky.
The small bell of mist, the singing of the waters from
    the mountains.
Dilijan, di-li-jan-di-li-jan-jan-jan-jan!
Silence…

Translated from Russian by Liz Page and David Matevossian.
* Dilijan is a town in the mountains covered with forests, in the north-east of
Armenia. "Jan" means "Dear", "Soul", "Beloved one;" in Armenia it is a way
to address someone beloved and important.

‖ *Romania* ‖

Liliana Ursu

Îmbătrânind

Îmi privesc mâinile,
încă nu s-au urâţit.
Ochii luminaţi de bucurii
ori de lacrimi
încă strălucesc.

Ziua mi-o împart în felii egale :
atît pentru ai mei,
atît pentru ceilalţi ţi celelalte,
bucătărie, redacţie, catedră,
caietul cu poezii,
în sfârşit grădina,
mormîntul părinţilor.

E primăvară.
Am cumpărat flori.
Din ce în ce mai mult
m-aplec peste ţărâna caldă,
mâinile mele o scormonesc,
o întreabă în timp ce înfig
firavele rădăcini de
nu mă uita.

Apoi scot apă
din fântîna morţilor.
Doar aici, în cimitirul Mânăstirii
mai au şi cei plecaţi la Domnul
ceva al lor.
Ud florile abia sădite,
mă îndrept de spate,
încerc să aprind o lumânare
dar vântul se hrăneşte lacom
cu flacăra ei.

Tot mîinile mele o păzesc,
mîinile mele pline de pământ,
aproape nu le mai recunosc.

Și grădina de acasă mă așteaptă
și florile ei vor apă și iubire.

Sigur mă voi ocupa de grădinărit
între două vârste,
între două feluri de mâncare,
o lecție despre poeții metafizici
și o imprimare la radio
dau fuga cu cu gândul în grădină
mîinile mi-o iau înainte,
tot mai aproape de pământ,
semn că îmbătrânesc.

O altfel de înțelepciune e acest joc cu pământul…

"Bucurați-vă!" le a spus Domnul femeilor Mironosițe
după Înviere lor li s-a arătat prima oară.

Și grădina și vântul, chiar și vârsta mea
îmi strigă : bucură-te, bucură-te,
bucură-te !

Liliana Ursu

Growing Old

I gaze at my hands, not yet
grown ugly. My eyes
still sparkle, brightened
by joys, jeweled
by tears.

I offer my days
in unequal portions:
so much for my family,
so much for other people and the usual demands–
the kitchen, the editorial office, teaching,
my notebook of poems.
Finally, the garden
and my parents' grave.

It's spring–
I've bought flowers to plant.
More and more often I find myself bending
to the warm earth, my hands
digging in its dust.
I press soil over the tender roots
of forget-me-nots.

Then, from the well of the dead,
I draw a pail of water.
Only here, near the convent,
do the dead still have something
to call their own.

I water the newly planted flowers,
then stand and stretch my back, bend
again, try to light a memorial candle.

When the wind feeds
on the tiny flame, I shelter it
with my cupped hands,
hands so soiled with earth
I barely recognize them. At home
my own garden waits,
its flowers also in need of water and love.

I'm convinced that between two moments of life,
between two bites of food,
I'll suddenly dedicate myself to gardening.
Between a lesson on metaphysics

and a recording session for my radio program,
I let my thoughts fly into that other garden.
But my hands, so much closer
to the earth, always get there
before me, a sign of my growing old.
This is my hide-and-seek
with the earth, another kind of wisdom...

"Rejoice!" God proclaimed to the holy women
when He first revealed Himself to them
after the Resurrection.

And the garden, and the wind—even the years
I've become—cry out to me. *Rejoice! Rejoice!*

---

*Translated from Romanian by Liliana Ursu, Adam J. Sorkin
and Tess Gallagher.*

|| *Russian Federation* ||

Yevgeny Yevtushenko

Счастье будет для всех, если ни на одну
Люди все на Земле не пойдут на войну

Divine Happiness knocks on your door
When you choose not to go to war.

Translated from Russian by Valerie Reeder.

Mutalip Beppaev

АЙ

Ай - ай - ай!...
Къалай жаланды ай:
Къышхыда
Къабыша, къалтырай,
Кёкню
Кёк бузунда учхалай,
Баргъан
Ай!.
Ай - ай - ай!...
Къалай жаланды ай:
От жагъа
Жылыугъа учханлай,
Мияла
Кёзлени къучакълай
Баргъан
Ай!...
Ай - ай - ай!...
Къалай жаланды ай:
Жылы жай...
Баллиде да жырлай,
Хар будай
Бюртюкден да къарай,
Баргъан
Ай!...
Ай - ай - ай!...
Къалай жаланды ай:
Къышхыда
Къабыша, къалтырай,
Кёкню
Кёк бузунда учхалай,
Баргъан
Ай!...

Mutalip Beppaev

Ah

Ah – ah – ah
What the naked moon
In the winter
Freezing and shivering
On the ice heavenly slipping
The moon is coming
Ah – ah – ah
What the naked moon
As flying to the warmth
Of the heart
As hugging
The glass eye
The moon is flying
Ah – ah – ah
What the naked moon
In the winter
Freezing and shivering
On the ice heavenly slipping
The moon is coming
Ah – ah – ah
What the naked moon
In the winter
Freezing and shivering
On the ice heavenly slipping
The moon is coming
Ah!...

Translated from Balkar by Iurii Moskalev and Sergey Scheglov.

Yury Entin

Прекрасное далёко

Слышу голос из прекрасного далёка,
Голос утренний в серебряной росе.
Слышу голос и манящая дорога
Кружит голову как в детстве карусель.

Прекрасное далёко
Не будь ко мне жестоко,
Не будь ко мне жестоко,
Жестоко не будь.
От чистого истока
В прекрасное далёко,
В прекрасное далёко
Я начинаю путь.

Слышу голос из прекрасного далёко,
Он зовет меня в чудесные края,
Слышу голос, голос спрашивает строго:
А сегодня что для завтра сделал я?

Я клянусь, что стану чище и добрее,
И в беде не брошу друга никогда.
Слышу голос – и спешу на зов скорее
По дороге, на которой нет следа.

Yury Entin

My Beautiful Tomorrow

A song

I can hear the voice from Beautiful Tomorrow,
It is calling like a silver jingle bell.
I can hear it in the middle of the road
And I'm happy and I'm letting out a yell!

Chorus
My Beautiful Tomorrow,
Don't bring me woe and sorrow,
Don't bring me woe and sorrow,
Don't hurt me so much!
Desire starts to grow,
I'm heading for Tomorrow,
I'm heading for Tomorrow,
I feel its magic touch.

I can hear the voice from Beautiful Tomorrow,
It's inviting me to visit wonder lands
I can hear it asking strictly if I know
What I've done today with my own head and hands.

Chorus

Now, I promise I will never be atrocious
And I won't desert my best friend in his need.
I can hear the voice, it's good to me and gracious
And I'm rushing to the sound I will meet.

Chorus

Andrey Korovin

море: лимонными дольками

нарежьте мне море лимонными дольками
без чаек отчаянья
море - и только
чтоб был ободок от восхода по краю
и быстрый дельфин как посланник из рая

и я под язык положу эту дольку
чтоб выжить зимою полынной и горькой
чтоб плавать зимою как рыба в воде
подобно морской путеводной звезде

Andrey Korovin

sea: lemon slices

cut into slices, the sea
without gulls of despair
sea and sea only
i want that rim of the sunrise over the edge
and a quick dolphin as a messenger from heaven

and I'll put this slice under the tongue
to survive bitter and wormwood winter
to swim in winter, like a fish in water
as a guiding star over the sea

Translated from Russian by German Vlasov.

Igor Shaferan

МЫ ЖЕЛАЕМ СЧАСТЬЯ ВАМ

В мире, где кружится снег шальной,

Где моря грозят крутой волной,

Где подолгу добрую ждём порой мы весть,

Чтобы было легче в трудный час,

Очень нужно каждому из нас,

Очень нужно каждому знать, что счастье есть.

Мы желаем счастья вам,

Счастья в этом мире большом!

Как солнце по утрам,

Пусть оно заходит в дом.

Мы желаем счастья вам,

И оно должно быть таким

Когда ты счастлив сам,

Счастьем поделись с другим.

В мире, где ветрам покоя нет,

Где бывает облачным расвет,

Где в дороге дальней нам часто снится дом,

Нужно и в грозу, и в снегопад,

Чтобы чей-то очень добрый взгляд,

Чей-то очень добрый взгляд согревал теплом.

Igor Shaferan

Happiness for Everyone!

A song

In the world where snow blocks up your way,

Where the oceans threaten with the wave,
Where we're waiting for good news every day and night.
So that you felt better in your need,
It is such a simple thing indeed,
It's essential that you know: Happiness exists.

Chorus
Happiness for everyone! Happiness in this giant world!
Like early rising sun, let it come into your home.
Happiness for everyone, but one thing it's better to know:
When happiness has come, don't be greedy, pass it on.

In the world, where winds do not calm down,
Where the sunrise only brings a frown,
Where in long and tiring journey, home – is what's our lead,
In cold winter or in midday sun
One necessity for everyone:
Just one tender smiling look warming with its heat.

Chorus
Happiness for everyone!
Happiness for everyone!
Happiness for everyone!
Happiness for everyone!

Set to music by Stas Namin (Anastas A. Mikoyan).

‖ *Serbia* ‖

Ljubivoje Ršumović

Na Detinjasto Pitanje

Na detinjasto pitanje
Kada sam napisao
Prvu pesmu
Odgovaram osmehom

Nisam još
Tekću
Sada pišem svoje
Poslednje pesme
Prvu ću napisati
Na kraju

Pašće Severnjača
U moju sobu
Da mi osvetli
Put olovci
I da otkravi
Moje samoljublje

Pisaću stojeći
Kao Hemingvej
Ne zbog lumbalnih
Smetnji
Već iz puke
Lirske učtivosti

Ljubivoje Ršumović

Childish Question

On a childish question
When I wrote
My first poem
I respond

I still haven't
But I will
Right now I am writing
My last poems
The first one will be written
In the end

The North Star will fall
Into my room
To light the way
To my pen
And to melt
My self-respect

I will write in a standing position
Like Hemingway
Not because of lumbar
Troubles
But out of sheer
Politeness

Translated from Serbian by Zoran Paunović.

|| *Slovenia* ||

Lucija Stupica

Ukradena Lepota

Prebudili smo se v blešč eč e jutro,
si umili zobe in posedli za mizo.
Dan se je šele zač enjal.
Zunaj so se razpirali oljč ni nasadi
in č loveške usode
kakor pisano perilo č ez
ogromno kamnito dvorišč e.
Vse, kar je kakor dolga,
poč asna glasba postalo
temna kulisa, se je svetlilo.
Podobe so bile moč nejše, več je od
drobne pisave, ujete med robove papirja.
Veter nas je zaprtih oč i zibal kakor barke,
limonovec ponujal temno zelena krila.
Sadili smo majhna in velika hotenja,
si dopisovali s pticami, ki so v mirnem letu
preletavale široke ceste tišine,
snemali filme v priprtih oč eh,
in č e si rekel: lep ali lepa si,
si rekel zato, ker si tako mislil.
Ko se je dan spušč al č ez ramena,
je bilo, kot da hodimo po prazni obali
in nas ljubkuje nebo. Spominjalo je
na Arkadijo, in bilo je blizu.
Poletje nas je izpihovalo
in oblikovalo v velike č aše,
polne mehkejših,
vse mehkejših misli.

Lucija Stupica

Stolen Beauty

We woke up into a shining morning,
brushed our teeth and sat down at the table.
The day had only just begun.
Outside, olive groves
and human destinies unfolded
like gaily coloured laundry over
a large stony backyard.
All that like long, slow music
turned into dark scenery, brightened.
Images were stronger, larger
than tiny writing caught between the paper's edges.
With our eyes closed, wind tossed us like barges,
a lemon-tree offered us dark green wings.
We were planting small and big desires,
writing letters to birds quietly
flying over the wide roads of silence,
shooting films in our barely open eyes,
and if you said you are beautiful,
you said it because you meant it.
As the day descended over our shoulders,
it was as if we had walked along an isolated beach,
caressed by the sky. It resembled
Arcadia and it was close.
Summer blew us out
moulding us into goblets
brimming with softer,
ever softer thoughts.

Translated from Slovene by Janko Lozar.

|| *Turkey* ||

Yeşim Ağaoğlu

buzlu şiir

buzda açan lale
buzda dönen mevlana
ak kuş
kara kartal
buz tutmuş kanatlar
rudolf'un ince bacakları
bir balerinin göğe açılan kolları
tanrıya giden buzlu yolda
boy vermiş dikenler
bir kuğunun buzlar üzerinde can çekişmesi
donmuş bir nilüferin cesedi
ve sen ne kadar sıcaksın
meydan okur gibi herşeye
sarkıtların dikitlerin ne kadar sıcak senin
gelsen de bütün buzlar erise

Yeşim Ağaoğlu

icy poem

ice blooming tulip
dervish whirling on ice
white falcon black eagle
wings frozen in ice
rudolf's slender legs
a ballerina's arms outstretched to the sky
thorns growing along
the icy path leading to god
a swan breathing his last on the ice
the body of an ice-drowned lily-of-the-pond,
while you, how very hot you are
as if challenging all things icy
how hot your stalactites and stalagmites
wish you were here so all the ice could melt

Translated from Turkish by Nihal Yeğinobalı.

|| *Ukraine* ||

Dmytro Lazutkin

РЯТУВАЛЬНІ ЧОВНИ І ВЕЖІ

Самотньо блукаючи пляжами на південному морі
натрапляєш на кинуті прапори і пожовклі трояндові листки

небесні вентилятори
розганяють холодне повітря
лишаючи спокій

мою війну закінчено
моє серце лежить під соснами

мої птахи літають над хвилями
не знаючи де їм сісти

стільки свободи
навколо
стільки свободи

Dmytro Lazutkin

Lifeboats and Lifeguard Stands

Strollingalonealong a southernsea
youstumbleuponforsakenflagsandrosepetalsyellowed

paradisalventilators
dispersethecoldair
leavingstillness

mywarhasbeenconcluded
myheartrestsbeneaththepines

mybirdshoverabovethewaves
notknowingwheretoland

somuchfreedom
allaround
somuchfreedom

Translated from Ukrainian by Mark Andryczyk and Andrij Kudla.

Greta Stoddart

You drew breath

as a boy draws something silver from a river,
an angler from the sea a bale of weed;
as a woman draws herself from a bath,
as blood is drawn from a vein.
You drew breath as thread is drawn through
the eye of a needle, wet sheets through a mangle,
as steel is drawn through a die to make wire
and oil draws up through wick its flag of fire.
You drew breath as a reservoir draws from a well
of ink and a mouth and a nose and eyes are drawn,
as a sheet is drawn from under the dying
and over the heads of the dead.
You drew breath as the last wheezing pint is drawn,
as money and a bow and the tide are drawn;
as up over her head a woman draws
a dress and down onto her a man.
You drew breath as a cloud draws its pall
across the moon, across the car park
where a sky-blue line draws the way
all the way to Maternity; as all in blue
they drew a semi-circle round the bed,
a line and then a knife across the skin;
as in another room someone drew
a curtain round its runner, a hand across
a pair of finished eyes. You drew breath
as they drew you – besmeared and blue – out
and sublime was your fury at being drawn
into this air, this theatre; you drew breath
for the first time – for a second I held mine.

Scotland

Sheena Blackhall

A Buddhist Valentine

I love the silence that invites the birds
To hop un-frightened round the open shrine

I love the heart that welcomes sky and earth
Where all things intermingle and combine

I love the mind that opens up to all
The lotus in the mud, whose petals shine

Alan Spence

Today

Today came spring
                    -ing
                          It
took me by surprise,
leapt and
bowled me over
like a big
daft dog,

on a train rolling through
snowcovered hills, the
bright sun scudding beside me
                              along
touching me awake to see.

Today it came
with crocuses open by
hardfrozen tractortracks
with daffodils, bent by the snow
but Trumpetting

with O the sun
and even, God, lambs
Today came Spring.

Wales

Menna Elfyn

Cerdd garegog

Carreg ddrws dy fodolaeth,
sy'n llechen lân y bore.

Maen ar gronglwyd f'enaid,
un cam wrth fur cariad
sy raid. Un syml, sownd.

Wnes i ddim deall helfa
pobl am risial, neu glap aur,
na deimwnt. Dim ond

diolch am y meini mewn llaw,
meini mellt weithiau o'r awyr,
maen sugn, dwy long mewn harbwr,

maen tynu atat synnwyr
a'r maen hir mewn oes o raean
fe dreigla heb fwsogli.

Maen hogi fy ymennydd,
meini cellt, yn mynnu tanchwa
dan feinwe'n chwarel grai.

Maen ar faen yn gerrig milltir
y cerddaf atynt yn llawen,
gan delori fel clap y cerrig.

Menna Elfyn

Stones

The doorstep of your being
is every morning's clean slate.

The capstone of my soul,
just one step and I set it
firm and true in the wall of love.

I never understood
the hunger for crystals, a nugget of gold,
a diamond. Just gave thanks

for the stones in my hand—
sometimes a thunderbolt straight from the sky,
a lodestone, two ships in harbour,

a magnet to draw the senses,
a menhir in an age of gravel:
it moves, without gathering moss.

The whetstone of my mind,
two flints striking a firestorm
to rage in the quarry of flesh that we mine.

Stone on stone, the milestones
I walk to gladly,
the spark in my heart like two stones singing.

Translated from Welsh by Elin ap Hywel.

LATIN AMERICA
and
THE CARIBBEAN

Photo: Jowan Gauthier

‖ *Argentina* ‖

Julia Enriquez

Me dijeron que debía asumir por mi cuenta el lenguaje entero

Tal vez respondí que sí con la cabeza o en voz alta
pero en verdad estaba repasando el relieve de mis dientes
con la lengua

estaba encajando mi cara en el rincón de la fachada
de algún hotel lujoso
o entornando la mirada para dejar las líneas
por fuera de sus focos

para dejar asegurado en algún lugar el engranaje fanático
de mis recuerdos
un baile lento entre lo no aprendido y las coincidencias
    felices
el sonido de mis sueños aclarándose
sobre el mar de la lucidez desobediente

Julia Enriquez

They told me I had to take over language all by myself

Maybe I answered yes by nodding or saying it out loud
but in fact I was going over the relief of my teeth
with my tongue

I was fitting my face in the corner of the façade
of some luxurious hotel
or half-closing my eyes so as to leave the lines
outside their focal points

so as to secure someplace the fanatic gears
of my memories
a slow dance between what I did not learn and all the
    happy coincidences
the sound of my dreams becoming clearer
above the sea of disobedient lucidity

|| *Barbados* ||

Kamau Brathwaite

She Gardening

for Pam Mordecai

She diggin a small hole this morning in the kitchen garden. for
the breadfruit shoot a farmer give her
weeding the weeds to plant her okro seeds and pour-

ing solstice water on their ground now that the drought
is lifting and the storms don't come as yet and her dark brown
arms begin to lose the signature of doubt upon their page
and the moisture on her namsetoura skin is sing & shine

We have come-through such hebby hebby times
and more much more is still in storieage
But for these small gestures in the sunwine warming
w/out worrying . praise to the Lord for these young shoots
who help & raise us up and bless us one more time

|| *Brazil* ||

Adriana Lisboa

Cafarnaum

Se não há messias
ou curandeiro à mão, dá um jeito
levanta-te e dança.
São poucos os que arriscam
neste momento – as
normas da compostura estão escritas
em letras garrafais na parede
mas finge que não viu.

Dá um jeito, pede licença
vai abrindo caminho
desvia das cartolas
das carolas das cartilhas
calibra
os teus pés forros à vertigem
e dança.

Adriana Lisboa

Capernaum

If there aren't any messiahs
or shamans around, improvise
rise and dance.
Few will take the risk
at this moment – the
norms of composure are written
in giant letters on the wall
but pretend you haven't seen them.

Improvise, excuse yourself
make your own way
avoid pep talks
primers pulpiteers
calibrate
your feet for giddiness, unimpeded
and dance.

Translated from Portuguese by Alison Entrekin.

|| *Chile* ||

Sergio Infante

La Dicha

Como los viejos gozadores
y no como los viejos glotones,
escribamos el destino.
Esperemos la sequedad final
a sabiendas de que un día
será el Día.
Tardemos en encontrarnos al Simurg
lejos del Árbol de la Ciencia y del nido:
el piojillo suplanta el fuego en las plumas;
el vuelo errante, a ras de miedo.
Retrasemos esas talas perentorias
cuidando lo que aún permanece.
Hay un goce en ello; un placer,
resistir lo inexorable a mano madrina.
Sin hartarse con ases en la manga.
Sin engullir grandezas que mañana
serán cerros de chatarra entre humaredas.
Dejemos de comernos el mundo a tarascones,
aplaquemos esas ganas de tragarlo de un bocado.
Acordemos paladearlo a cucharadas lentísimas
como si fuera un postre irrepetible,
más que ningún otro, deleitoso.

Sergio Infante

Bliss

Like the old enjoyers
and not like the old gluttons,
let us write fate.
Let us wait for the final dryness
knowing full well that one day
will be The Day.
Let's not hurry to the meeting with the Simurg
far from the Tree of Knowledge and from the nest:
the red mites forge the fire in the feathers;
the wandering flight, bordering fear.
Let us delay these peremptory fellings
taking care of that which still remains.
There is enjoyment in it; a pleasure,
to resist the inexorable with the hand of a godmother.
Without stuffing ourselves with aces in the sleeve.
Without gulping grandeurs that tomorrow
will be hills of scrap among clouds of smoke.
Let's no longer eat the world with big bites,
let us appease the desire to swallow it in one bite.
Let us agree on tasting it in very slow spoonfuls
as if it were a unique dessert,
more than any other, delightful.

Translated from Spanish by Tamara A. Strugo.

|| *Dominican Republic* ||

Rei Berroa

Utilidades De La Risa

Desde ques mar el agua,
desde ques tiempo el ahora
y desde ques también vida el sueño
con sus verticales coordenadas
de llanto y de ternura,
sus horizontales herramientas
de alivio y de dolor,
de lo real amarilleando
entre lo espeso y lo flüido,

la risa

ha puesto sus huevos en la arena
movediza de la lengua,
estruendosa se dispara por los huecos
bien abiertos de la boca y el gaznate,
arruga las esquinas de los ojos, los obliga
a prestarle atención al desahogo,
se hincha imprevisible en los carrillos,
en las narices del barro en el que estamos contenidos,
nos libera de la ira y del espasmo de la hora
y nos saca de los miedos en que quieren que vivamos
los que ostentan el poder y lo blanden
ante el ojo del votante o parroquiano.

Aunque dure solamente
unos minúsculos segundos destilados
a esta frágil existencia que parece interminable,
la conciencia de la risa
fortalece las paredes en que habita nuestro pulso,
nos ablanda el nervio adolorido de la angustia,

Rei Berroa

The Usefulness of Laughter

Since water is sea,
since now is time
and since sleep is also life
with its vertical coordinates
of tears and tenderness,
its horizontal tools
of pain and relief,
reality yellowing
between thick and thin,

laughter

lays its eggs
in the tongue's shifting sand,
shoots thunderously through
apertures of mouth and gullet,
wrinkles the corners of eyes,
forces them to pay attention to relief,
swells the cheeks without warning,
right in the face of the clay we're made of,
it frees us from rage and from the spasm of time,
removes us from the fears those in power
want to immerse us in, brandishing themselves
before parishioner's or voter's eyes.

Even if it only lasts
a few distilled and miniscule seconds
of fragile existence that can seem interminable,
a consciousness of laughter
fortifies the walls of the house our pulse inhabits,

las terribles soledades que sufrimos a veces sin saberlo,
le quita máscaras al río crecido del orgullo,
nos descuajaringa, corta la ceguera irreductible
que marchita la flor del loto en la laguna
y a su modo nos lima sutilmente a los humanos,
todas las aristas del cuerpo y de la idea,
del tiempo y de las mañas que maneja cuando pasa.

Antídoto que limpia de inmundicias las arterias de la vida,
la etapa de la risa es señal inconfundible
de que es el hombre, no los hados o el omnipotente,
quien fabrica los telares de su propia humanidad.

Por ello, no hay que fiarse nunca de los dioses
que no quieren o no saben o no pueden reír o sonreír
aunque sólo sea por un breve instante iluminado.

weakens the pained nerve of anguish,
the terrible loneliness we sometimes suffer
without even knowing we do,
it removes the masks of pride's raging river,
shatters us to bits, cuts through the permanent blindness
that withers the lotus flower on the lake
and in its own way subtly shapes us humans,
all the edges of body and idea,
of time and how it signals its passage.

Antidote that cleanses filth from life's arteries,
the stage of laughter is the perfect sign
that it is humans, not fate or the omnipotent,
who weave the quilt of our humanity.

> Which is why we must never trust the gods
> who don't want or know how to laugh or smile
> even for a single illuminated moment.

Translated from Spanish by Margaret Randall and Rei Berroa.

Ángela Hernández Núñez

La abeja

La abeja
Chupa el alba
Es primavera.

The Bee

The Bee
Sucks at the dawn
It is Spring.

Translated from Spanish by Tanya Uluwitiya.

Norberto James

(Re)posesión

Son míos esta luz chata del mediodía,
esta brisa blanda, jugetona,
los callados y extensos flamboyanes,
las guajanas enhiestas y orgullosas,
la guásima diseñadora de sombras,
el jabillo tronante,
el impávido guayacán,
acuchillando unos,
frotando otros,
los invisibles bordes del día,
su bóveda impalpable,
su copioso esplendor.
Míos son estos pastos,
estas tierras, aquellas montañas,
su estirada y muda deposición de siglos,
arroyuelos y ríos en su anegada danza de burbujas,
y guijarros pulidos por la espera.
¡Todo es mío!

Norberto James

(Re)possession

Mine, the flat light at midday,
this tender, playful breeze,
the hushed vast expanses of flamboyant trees,
cane flowers upright and proud,
the guásima tree, creator of tropical shadows,
the thundering sandbox tree,
the fearless guaiacum,
some trees stabbing,
others rubbing away
the invisible edges of the day,
its untouchable vaulted canopy,
its copious splendor.
Mine, these meadows,
these lands, those mountains
and their mute testimony spanning the centuries,
brooks and rivers in a flooded dance of bubbles
and pebbles made smooth from waiting.
All is mine!

Translated from Spanish by Beth Wellington.

|| *El Salvador* ||

Javier Zamora

Si Fuera

Para Monseñor Romero

Hoy bendigan: hojas trepándose en arboles, cenizas
lavadas de las aceras, y los nombres anotados

en el desfile de los "aparecidos." Ya no hay guerra:
pájaros carpinteros taladran madera seca, estudiantes

gritan sus propios nombres—las rosas de las rosas
creciendo en sus bocas. Bendigan la sequilla de balas,

el remedio del cholera, y el consuelo de terremotos. Ya no hay
casamientos entre anillos de seguridad y cráteres. Bendigan

todas las cosas que no sabíamos amar: exiliados, cielos-callados,
buses, caminatas de medianoche, radios, y petardos. Bendigan

techos de lamina, cañales en llamas, y cocos cantando:
y aquí que solo pensábamos en pérdidas. Bendigan las M-16s

rendidas y soportadas por artillería oxidada. Ya no hay nada
que los recuerde de botas marchando, como si fueran lluvia.

Javier Zamora

If It Were

For Monseñor Romero

Bless today, leaves crawling back on trees, ashes
washed from sidewalks, and the collecting of names

at the "appeared" parade. No more war: woodpeckers
probe deadwood, students shout their own names—

the roses of roses growing in mouths. Bless
the drought of bullets, cured cholera, and the comfort

of earthquakes. No more marriages between safety-pins
and craters. Bless all things we didn't know we loved:

exiles, silent-skies, buses, midnight walks, radios,
firecrackers. Bless tin rooftops, cane burning,

and palms singing: here, we only thought of loss. Bless
the surrendered M-16s propped next to rusting

artillery. There's nothing left that reminds us
of the marching of boots, as if it were rain.

Translated from Spanish to English by Javier Zamora.

‖ *Haiti* ‖

Michèle Voltaire Marcelin

Sezon Printan

Men kijan lanmou kòmanse
Sezon printan louvri ak non-w
Polènn poudre tout flè dore
Tout fey mele koulè vèt melanje
nan sant la pli ki finn tonbe
Pwason glise tankou lang nan bouch
La nati fleri
toulimen nan sezisman.

Translated from English to Haitian Creole by Michèle Voltaire Marcelin.

Michèle Voltaire Marcelin

Springtime

This is the way that Love began
Spring opened with your name
With pollen-powdered flowers
and leaves tangled green
in the after-scent of rain
Fish flowed as freely as kisses
All bloomed
luminous and startling.

Juan Felipe Herrera

Happiness Each Time

On the corner of my house
With unknown light with unknown music
It is   one tree
Inside I reach   up
To the infinite sound

Ten thousand conversations
Sparrows tiny rough elders of the village
My wings my wings! They nod at each other
So many things so many languages

Listen to the Dalai Lama
Let us celebrate Ghandi's Anniversary he says
So he speaks
                    Of non-violence
                              So he speaks

Of right view right effort
          It is enough to be kind
                    Everything else is extra
How can you be non-violent in times of assault?
One Indian student says under the unraveling sun

How can you even pronounce the word *peace*
                              In a forest of bullets
Violence   multiplies it doesn't know   patience
His Holiness the Dalai Lama laughs
It is the laughter of a wisdom-child

A poet needs to see things the world
As it settles into your hands

In the leafy market place
Among the silvery fish ask them
What are you doing here?
Fly with them back to the breath of the sea
Over the green striped boats
Down through the rings of algae come
Back up
Now look back

Happiness is the heart-shaped tree
It is the Indian student under the complete sky
It is you it is the fish we saved
Waiting to fly back home
                        It is the infinite sound

Raquel Lubartowski

˙agio a Idea Vilariño
Borges

˙o al legado borgeano

˙lementos:
el oscuro azul

o será una risa leve
una habitación de hotel.

es duelan
las camisetas de algodón
o naufrague en aquel *lejano infancia paraíso cielo*
ya sé que entre los días futuros
habrá uno,
solo uno
y será el primero.

Raquel Lubartowski

A Plagiarism of Idea Vilariño and J.L. Borges

Today I renounce the Borgesian legacy
and will be happy
with the four elements:
Eros, Thanatos and the dark blue
of your gaze.
The fourth element will be an easy laugh
at the lip of a hotel room.
Today I renounce
unhappiness
and even though sometimes
cotton shirts may ache
or we shipwreck in that *distant childhood paradise sky*
I know that among future days
there will be one,
just one
and it will be the first one.

Translated from Spanish by Carolina De Robertis.

NORTH
AMERICA

Photo: Abedan Solomon

Nora Atalla

Le Chant de la Vie

si dans une larme luisait le regard
de l'enfance béate
si dans l'océan flottaient les caresses
de la menotte tendue au soleil
la vie continuerait son chant
dans la chaleur des rayons
le cœur se gonflerait de bourgeons

et voilà le ronflement des lendemains
avec les promesses d'arcs-en-ciel
à emporter sur les chemins inexplorés

Nora Atalla

The Song of Life

if a tear glistened in the eyes
of blissful childhood
if in the ocean floated caresses
of the child's hand stretched toward the sun
in the warm rays
life would continue its song
buds would swell in the heart

and here would come tomorrows purring
with promises of rainbows
to carry upon unexplored paths

Translated from French by Nora Atalla.

Jean Désy

Dans une Tente dans la Toundra
(Tupirmi Nunatuinami)

Onze amis réunis
Dans une tente dans la toundra
Le soir et les enfants tendres
Collés aux genoux des mangeurs de viande
De la neige sur la tente
Et tant d'autres neiges mêlées aux lichens
Des aurores de ciel boréal
Molles et vanillées roulées aux noirceurs
Comme si toutes les neiges
Voulaient danser sur une fresque
Dans une tente dans la toundra
Le soir et onze amis réunis
Autour d'assiettes cliquetantes
L'odeur violette des réchauds
Et du mouillé des chandails de laine
Quand les uns osent parler d'harmonie
Alors que partout ailleurs dans le monde
Il y a tant d'attente et d'impatience
Onze dans la nuit ensorcelée
Par les tornades d'ionosphère
Et les rires d'un enfant chatouillé
Les chants d'un homme enivré
Par les fous rires des autres âmes
Tandis qu'une femme silencieuse
Berce dans son dos l'univers
Et qu'au-dehors passent les yeux
De renards et de rats musqués
Onze amis dans une tente
Réchauffent la toundra de leurs rires
Et les appels d'un homme chaviré
Qui crie mon amour mon amour
À l'enfant qui sourit

Jean Désy

In a Tent on the Tundra
(Tupirmi Nunatuinami)

Eleven friends together
In a tent on the tundra
One night with loving children
Hanging onto the meat eaters' knees
Snow on the tent
And so many other snows mixed with lichen
Auroras in the boreal sky
Soft and vanilla-scented rolled into the darkness
As if all snows
Wanted to dance on a fresco
In a tent on the tundra
One night and eleven friends together
Around rattling dishes
The purple smell of stoves
And the wetness of woollen sweaters
People daring to talk about harmony
When everywhere in the world
There is so much impatience
Eleven in the night bewitched
By ionospheric tornados
And the giggles of a tickled newborn
The songs of a man drunk on
The laughter of the other souls
While a silent woman
Rocks the universe on her back
And outside roam the eyes
Of foxes and muskrats
Eleven friends in a tent
Warm up the tundra with laughter
And calls from a capsized man
Saying my love my love
To a newborn who smiles

Translated from French by Jean Désy.

Jacques Ouellet

À Lili

Retiens-moi de l'effraction du vertige   ne m'échappe pas
Blottie dans la force de ton amour
Garde-moi de basculer dans l'espérance et la ferveur du lait
Qu'encore si petite
Je reconnaisse la lenteur pacificatrice de tes grands bras
Tout doucement papa   berce-moi

For Lili

Hold me afar from the whirl of vertigo   don't let me slip away
Nestled in the strength of your love quiet me down
Keep me from falling into the expectations and fervour of milk
So as small as I may be
I shall recognize the pacifying slowness of your arms
So lightly papa   cradle me

Translated from French by Sylvie Nicolas.

Michel Pleau

Les Matins d'éternité

quand je souffle sur la flamme
une fleur tremblante me quitte
beau souvenir trop lent
pour se tenir debout

mais qu'ils sont doux les matins d'éternité
quand les rêves tremblent encore
dans la simplicité des gestes
et l'accomplissement des fruits

alors je sors de moi

dehors la lumière
est un ancien parfum
devenu désir

il fait un temps de feuillage fou
penché sur le début des choses

Michel Pleau

The Mornings of Eternity

when I blow on the flames
a trembling flower leaves me
beautiful memory
too slow to stand

but they are sweet the mornings of eternity
when dreams tremble again
in the simplicity of movements
and the fulfilment of fruits

then I go out of myself

outside the light
is an ancient perfume
become desire

it is a time of crazy foliage
bending over the beginning of things

Translated from French by Howard Scott.

Priscila Uppal

Good Things

Slip under the door
and I will help you tie
the square knot your father taught you
on your last camping trip.

On the far left wall
is a portrait of a piano.
Take three steps back
and fine handwriting will appear–
a note from your first love
wishing to hear how you sound.

Open the cupboards in the kitchen
and in every cracker box and soup can
filled to the brim
is all the loose change you've
ever lost or given away.

Lift the duvet in the bedroom.
There lies the word on the tip of your tongue
the scent of your mother's hair
the bright bell of a new year.

The lights wane, but I am floating
like a feather above you. Lie down.
Stay awhile. Please. Let yourself
believe that every so often
good things happen.

Nilpushpi White

Silk

In the north of Cambodia, far from
      The rustle of tourists
clamoring over the ancient temples
        of Angkor,
Stand ceiling-high looms
Threaded with rainbow silks.
These will transform the offerings of
      tiny silk worms into fabric
        fit for kings.
Like that, our sweetest thoughts
      and kindest actions together
        create their own miracles.
Ah, and when we glimpse that
      majestic fabric of life and its
        intricate mirage of patterns and colors,
What joy, what happiness
      shimmers on the
simple backdrop of our lives!

Meena Alexander

Water Table

A river flows under my window
on its surface, I set a table.
Legs underwater, the tabletop rocks,
birds flock to watch:

 I lay a basket of eggs on the table
speckled rounds, polished with silk,
I set a bowl of milk
two mangoes freckled pink

 I set sleep on that table, dreams
and all the yearning that ever welled up
streaked with indigo from the fields
of Champaran, long grained rice,
roots blue as steel.

 Under the shadow of my hands
the table shifts on heavy water
I cry to those I love:
I have set a table for you,
come, come, quick!

Dara Barnat

Prayer for Happiness Found If You Cannot

For A.

let it be the curve of a letter in your name
let it be the sound of a language you don't understand
let it be the edge of a frayed blanket
let it be a dandelion seed floating over the earth
let it be grass growing through concrete
let it be a small strength in your own body
let it be thunder that can't touch you
let it be a fear that you struck down
let it be the person that brings you comfort, whoever they are
let it be the day you threw your head back with laughter
let it be the day you cried and didn't care
let it be sand on the beach that covered you
let it be an heirloom tomato with salt
let it be the night you were unafraid to dance
let it be white light or music or silence
let it be a star in the sky, even the weakest one
let it be the tip of the beak of a sparrow
let it be an ocean, a lake, a pond
let it be the water that drips from the faucet, giving you life

Richard Blanco

One Today

One sun rose on us today, kindled over our shores,
peeking over the Smokies, greeting the faces
of the Great Lakes, spreading a simple truth
across the Great Plains, then charging across the Rockies.
One light, waking up rooftops, under each one, a story
told by our silent gestures moving behind windows.

My face, your face, millions of faces in morning's mirrors,
each one yawning to life, crescendoing into our day:
pencil-yellow school buses, the rhythm of traffic lights,
fruit stands: apples, limes, and oranges arrayed like rainbows
begging our praise. Silver trucks heavy with oil or paper—
bricks or milk, teeming over highways alongside us,
on our way to clean tables, read ledgers, or save lives—
to teach geometry, or ring-up groceries as my mother did
for twenty years, so I could write this poem for us today.

All of us as vital as the one light we move through,
the same light on blackboards with lessons for the day:
equations to solve, history to question, or atoms imagined,
the "I have a dream" we keep dreaming,
or the impossible vocabulary of sorrow that won't explain
the empty desks of twenty children marked absent
today, and forever. Many prayers, but one light
breathing color into stained glass windows,
life into the faces of bronze statues, warmth
onto the steps of our museums and park benches
as mothers watch children slide into the day.

One ground. Our ground, rooting us to every stalk
of corn, every head of wheat sown by sweat
and hands, hands gleaning coal or planting windmills
in deserts and hilltops that keep us warm, hands
digging trenches, routing pipes and cables, hands
as worn as my father's cutting sugarcane
so my brother and I could have books and shoes.

Richard Blanco

Hoy, Uno

Un mismo sol hoy, encendido sobre nuestras costas,
se asoma sobre las Smokies, saluda las caras
de los Grandes Lagos, difunde una simple verdad
a través de las Grandes Llanuras, luego a la carga por las Rocosas.
Una misma luz despierta los techos: debajo de cada uno, un cuento
de nuestros gestos que se mueven, callados, detrás de las ventanas.

Mi rostro, tu rostro, millones en los espejos de la mañana,
cada uno bostezando a la vida, culminando en nuestro día:
camiones de escuela amarillo lápiz, el ritmo de los semáforos,
puestos de fruta: manzanas, limones, y naranjas surtidos como arcoíris
suplican nuestros elogios. Carreteras rebosando de camiones plata
cargados con aceite o papel, ladrillos o leche, junto a nosotros.
Vamos de camino a limpiar mesas, a leer registros o a salvar vidas—
a enseñar geometría, o atender la caja registradora como lo hizo mi madre
durante veinte años, para que yo pudiera escribirles este poema hoy.

Cada uno de nosotros tan vital como la luz única que atravesamos
la misma luz en los pizarrones con las lecciones del día:
ecuaciones por resolver, historia por cuestionar, o átomos imaginados,
el "Yo tengo un sueño" que seguimos soñando,
o el vocabulario imposible de la tristeza que no explica
los pupitres vacíos de veinte niños ausentes
hoy, y para siempre. Muchas plegarias pero una misma luz
inhala color a los vitrales,
sopla vida a las caras de las estatuas, y calienta
los escalones de nuestros museos y bancas del parque
mientras las madres observan a los niños adentrarse en el día.

Una misma tierra. Nuestra tierra, nos arraiga a cada tallo
de maíz, a cada espiga de trigo sembrados con sudor
y manos, manos que cosechan carbón o plantan molinos de viento
en los desiertos y las colinas para darnos calor, manos
que cavan zanjas, trazan tuberías y cables, manos

The dust of farms and deserts, cities and plains
mingled by one wind—our breath. Breathe. Hear it
through the day's gorgeous din of honking cabs,
buses launching down avenues, the symphony
of footsteps, guitars, and screeching subways,
the unexpected song bird on your clothes line.

Hear: squeaky playground swings, trains whistling,
or whispers across café tables, Hear: the doors we open
for each other all day, saying: hello/ shalom/
buon giorno/ namaste/ or buenos días
in the language my mother taught me—in every language
spoken into one wind carrying our lives
without prejudice, as these words break from my lips.

One sky: since the Appalachians and Sierras claimed
their majesty, and the Mississippi and Colorado worked
their way to the sea. Thank the work of our hands:
weaving steel into bridges, finishing one more report
for the boss on time, stitching another wound
or uniform, the first brush stroke on a portrait,
or the last floor on the Freedom Tower
jutting into a sky that yields to our resilience.

One sky, toward which we sometimes lift our eyes
tired from work: some days guessing at the weather
of our lives, some days giving thanks for a love
that loves you back, sometimes praising a mother
who knew how to give, or forgiving a father
who couldn't give what you wanted.

We head home: through the gloss of rain or weight
of snow, or the plum blush of dusk, but always, always
home, always under one sky, our sky. And always
one moon like a silent drum tapping on every rooftop
and every window, of one country—all of us—
facing the stars. Hope—a new constellation waiting
for us to map it, waiting for us to name it—together.

Translated from Spanish to English by Richard Blanco.

tan gastadas como las de mi padre que cortaban caña
para que mi hermano y yo tuviéramos libros y zapatos.

El polvo de nuestras granjas y desiertos, ciudades y planicies
mezclado por un mismo viento—nuestro aliento. Respira.
   Escúchalo
en el hermoso estruendo del día: los taxis y su claxon,
autobuses disparados por las avenidas, la sinfonía
de los pasos, guitarras y el chirrido del metro,
el inesperado pájaro cantor en tu tendedero.

Escucha: columpios chillones, trenes que silban,
o murmullos en los cafés. Escucha: las puertas
que abrimos todo el día: hello/ shalom/
buon giorno/ namaste/ o buenos días
en el idioma que mi madre me enseñó—en todos los idiomas
hablados al mismo viento que lleva nuestras vidas sin
prejuicio, mientras estas palabras parten de mis labios.

Un mismo cielo: desde que los Apalaches y las Sierras reclamaron
su majestad, y el Misisipí y el Colorado labraron
su camino hasta el mar. Agradece el trabajo de nuestras manos:
que tejen el hierro en puentes, terminan un reporte más
para el jefe, cosen otra herida o uniforme, la primer pincelada
de un retrato, el último piso de la Torre de la Libertad
resaltado en un cielo que cede ante nuestra resiliencia.

El mismo cielo hacia el cual a veces levantamos la mirada,
cansados de trabajar: unos días adivinamos el clima
de nuestra vida, otros días agradecemos un amor
que nos ama de vuelta, unas veces alabamos a una madre
que supo darnos más que todo, otras veces perdonamos
a un padre que no pudo dar lo que queríamos.

Volvemos a casa: a través del brillo de la lluvia, o el peso
de la nieve, o el rubor del atardecer, pero siempre, siempre
a casa, siempre debajo de ese cielo, nuestro cielo. Y siempre
una misma luna como tambor callado golpeteando en todos los techos
y en cada ventana de un país—todos nosotros—
de cara a las estrellas. La esperanza—una nueva constelación aguarda
que la tracemos, aguarda que la nombremos—juntos.

Sharon Dolin

If Happiness is Luck

the happenstance of you
the hap of us
now how get to the haptic
hush of us   the to-be-
touched   (so left to chance)
if lips will more than

if hips   to find bliss in the slipped
moment   how happed upon
we are   I say we when
you and me so shift-
ing are these I might get free

to bewilder in the wilderness of me

so remonstranced in romance
(do we bristle) how hap turns to hopeless how to make a haply
out of this now and this
and this   I ope my heart
too readily   my haptic heart

my hope sometime betimes mishap
Oh am I become Mis(s)Hap   are you the to-be-
missed happening   my backward glance   my sigh
within why (not)
to be a we   to happen in this instance
upon our stance (our happenstance) happily

Mark Doty

Pescadero

The little goats like my mouth and fingers,

and one stands up against the wire fence, and taps on the
   fence-board
a hoof made blacker by the dirt of the field,

pushes her mouth forward to my mouth,
so that I can see the smallish squared seeds of her teeth,
   and the bristle-whiskers,

and then she kisses me, though I know it doesn't mean "kiss,"

then leans her head way back, arcing her spine, goat yoga,
all pleasure and greeting and then good-natured indifference:
She loves me,

she likes me a lot, she takes interest in me, she doesn't
   know me at all
or need to, having thus acknowledged me. Though I am
   all happiness,

since I have been welcomed by the field's small envoy,
   and the splayed hoof,
fragrant with soil, has rested on the fence-board beside
   my hand.

Fady Joudah

Twice A River

After studying our faces for months
My son knows to beam
Is the thing to do

He'll spend years deciphering love
The injustice or the illusion
Having been brought into this world
Volition is an afterthought

What will I tell him
About land and language and burial
Places my father doesn't speak of
Perhaps my mother knows

In the movie the dispossessed cannot return
Even when they're dead
The journalist felt

Rebuke for not having thought
It mattered or for having thought it mattered too much

Will I tell my son all nations arise after mass
Murder that I don't know

Any national anthem by heart can't sing
Take Me Out to the Ball Game?

I should turn to flowers and clouds instead
Though this has already been said well
It is night

When he gazes
Into his mother's eyes at bath time
Qaiss & Laila she announces after a long day's work

He giggles with his shoulders not knowing
He's installing a web

In his amygdala or whichever
Places science thinks love dwells

Even love is a place? O son
Love no country and hate none
And remember crimes sometimes

Immortalize their victims
Other times the victimizer

Remember how you used to gaze at the trampoline
Leaves on their branches?

Don't believe the sound of the sea
In a seashell believe the sea
The endless trope and don't say

Much about another's language
Learn to love it

While observing silence
For the dead and the living in it.

Mahiruha Klein

Lullaby

Appalachian silver,
The rarest vein,
You shine on the roots
Of the mountains,
You lighten the burdens
Of the travelers
With your
Unspoken beauty.
O far-wandering troubadour,
Your ballads,
Like scarlet leaves
On the vast
Mississippi,
Shimmer through the paradox
Of human time
And then resound
Like the legends of God
In the Prairie,
And they suggest
The miraculous:
The last awakening
Of the Renaissance-Tree.
You are yourself
The first orchid
In the darkening forest,
The patience
Of the whispering leaves
And the delight
In the cold grass.

You visit us
With sheaves of madrigals,
Pristine as the stars,
And reminiscent of the soul,
The hopeless whistler,
The vagabond with flowers
Whom we despised
But you approached him,
And pressed
His melody to your heart.
In the mid-Summer light,
You cradle violets
In the hollow of your hands
And remind us that daisies
Are enough
To crown our children.
When painters barter
Their colors for cinnamon
And the jugglers sit
At the feet
Of the fiddlers,
We shall meet you again,
Renaissance Dreamer,
In the fullness
Of God's flowering Eye,
Merciful Feet
And "Good Morning"
Sun-burnished Heart.

Yusef Komunyakaa

With My Fish-Skin Drum

I shall sing the caravan home again,
bone & muscle holding me together,
earth & sky beneath my feet,

my fingers on the tablah, a red lotus
opening into the Great Rift Valley
till I am called to the reed boats.

I shall sing the whiskered tern's
lament I stole for occidental nights
as villagers walk toward big cities.

The caravan swallows the dust
of those before, woven into a dance
caught in a glow of night fires,

& I hold to my drum, waking voices
under the singing skin, the shish & tap
of fish skin on waters of a lost road.

Andréana Lefton

Learning to Pray

The room is cast in blue-green shadow
and outside the window a bird sings in a tree.

I am a small child. My mother
is kneeling. I go to her, and press myself

against her spine. I feel the prayers winging
through each vertebra. The moon

is a pearl in the sky. I do not know
how long we stay like this. The room

becomes the tree outside the window,
and the bird is now perched

on a turquoise dish holding stones
from Persepolis, Shiraz.

The darker it becomes, the better
I can see. The walls are shifting leaves

and the floor is a nest, a cradle,
an open palm. My mother cannot tell

if she is awake or dreaming. I close
my eyes and try to match my breath

to the ebb and flow of her ocean's tide.
I challenge my heart to beat

in time to the ground I rest
my cheek against. It is no use –

ungoverned heart. Together like this,
learning to pray, yet universes apart.

The bird flies away. The moon polishes itself
to a grain of sand that dissolves in the clear

forest pond we are kneeling in, rib to spine.
Time stops. Light braids into calligraphy.

This must be paradise, I think.

And without a word passing between us,
I feel my mother's bones say

It is.

Laren McClung

Gratitude

This morning I will not eat bread, eggs, or milk.
No tea or coffee, nothing tart or sweet.
Instead I awaken the gods with yogurt & honey,
offer frankincense, nightshade, & coconut water
before three times touching my hand to flame.
This is another way of turning oneself back
when the day otherwise turns toward the world.
From the fire escape the early morning eastern light
catches along the silvery underside of leaves
& wind spirals to animate the downward branches
of the willow until the tendrils perform a moody sway
& there, from within its motion, as if man or buffalo,
the whole tree gazes until I've been fully seen
& greens of late-summer tussle in the blustery air.
How lucky to be so thirsty when the clouds are full.

Naomi Shihab Nye

Small Basket of Happiness

It would never call your name.
But it would be waiting somewhere close,
perhaps under a crushed leaf
turned from pale green to gold
with no fanfare.
You hadn't noticed
the gathered hush
of a season's tipping.
Shadows flowing past
before any light came up,
people whom only a few
might remember,
so much accompaniment
inside a single breeze.
All whom we loved.
In their quiet passing lived
the happiness they had given.
And would still give, if only.
You would slow down a minute.
You would bend.

Emmy Pérez

For My Daughter, upon Losing the Startle Reflex

No more falling through
    the trees

        in the middle of the night.
           No need to grasp

            for leaves
               or my hair

        not there

      like we'd left
        for other bosques

          while you slept.

Who or what made it
    feel good
      to eat

        and sleep
          before Popocatépetl

            blows ash
      like snow?

The earth, right now,
    my love, is warm
      and snow-capped.

      Who or what
        made it so

          it feels good?

Jeffrey Yang

What Is

or is as true as
Happiness

Birth
A pure river

Conditions for the equal good
to be as wise and fortunate

at the start

Lost in the pursuit

Under a white oak
two children sitting back
to back on a plank swing, calling

The hand
that touches the earth
to witness

Presses the metal latch, opens
the screen door out from home

sunlight, pond water silence
damselfly at rest on a frond

Having come with you
this far into the drafty air

Jeffrey Yang

什么是

或真谛何是之
幸福

诞生
一道澄澈之河

分毫不差的优势
作为睿智和幸运

开始时

追逐里迷途

白橡树下
两个孩子背对
着背荡秋千，叫喊

那触摸大地
之手
要见证

按下金属插销，从屋内
打开纱门

阳光，池塘水静默
蕨叶上蜻蜓落定

与你同抵
这样深入凉风里

Translated from English to Mandarin by Liang Xiaoman.

OCEANIA

Photo: Robyn Sauer

‖ *Australia* ‖

Judith Beveridge

The Fishermen

After Stanley Moss

They have always reminded me
of lace-makers. The way they stand
at the shore, looking at the sea
as if it is an open page of knots,
never a closed fabric stitched
by needles. And the way they stand
as if darning a yacht, a bird,
distant waves breaking in circles,
the passages the moon takes out
through the cliffs.
                In their baskets
are things found in the hands
of needleworkers, haberdashers.
And see how they sit in the garnet
dusk, running threads into eyelets—
then bringing them back
and exposing an intimate dark.
And how they love the moon
in a scandalous design—as if
they were assured that the night
would not end without rapture
or the meridians of paradise.
                And see how they
breathe out clouds of cold, the sea
bunched about their wrists in cuffs;
how they take the white spray
like skeins to their fingers,
reading it for the spinnaker of a fish,
for the storm in an eyelet,

for the music sewn in like pearls,
for gulls flying out from the dunes.

       In a chivalry
of lines they listen to the sea,
to the shells, to their reels click
in amethyst quiet; to Odysseus
step out of the water shawled
in their sunstone-coloured nets,
his hand on his heart in a gesture
of disclosure, only the moon now
offering them sight over the waves,
as they too lift their arms into the sky.

Mark Tredinnick

Skipping the Rope

For Lucy

Just this, then: a girl in blue pyjamas—
Her small legs crossed at the ankles,
Her bare feet re-arranging winter
Into arabesques on the kitchen floor,
And she turns a rope, finer than spider's
Web, over (and over) her head, and jumps,
As it sweeps, like nothing at all, the floor
Boards clean beneath her feet. She lifts off
Twice between rotations, chanting some
Absent-minded rhyming fairy banter,
Rehearsing at light-speed who she is, becoming
The world's most nimble feather
Weight, the prettiest boxer there ever
Will be, while she waits for her toast to rise.

Closing

সদা সুসঙ, হিয়া বিহঙ,
তনু তরঙ, প্রাণ বিভঙ,
মন অভঙ, আশা সুড়ঙ।

Always what we need is good company.
Always what we need is the bird of our heart.
Always what we need is a divine wave
Flowing through our body.
Always what we need is beauty's varied
Expressions.
Always what we need is an undivided mind.
Always what we need is a hope-channel.

–Sri Chinmoy

Sri Chinmoy set to music his Bengali poem and translated it into English.

BIOGRAPHIES

ADONIS is an award-winning Syrian poet and essayist who led the modernist movement in Arabic poetry in the second half of the twentieth century. He has written more than twenty books in his native Arabic, including the pioneering work *An Introduction to Arab Poetics*.

YEŞİM AĞAOĞLU lives in İstanbul. She is a poet and contemporary artist, and President of the Turkish PEN Women Writers Committee. She has published nine books of poetry, and her poems have been translated into many other languages.

JIM PASCUAL AGUSTIN (Philippines) moved to Cape Town, South Africa, in 1994. Recent books of poetry include *Kalmot ng Pusa sa Tagiliran* (poems in Filipino, 2013) and *Sound Before Water* (poems in English, 2013). A new poetry collection, *A Thousand Eyes*, and a short story collection in Filipino are forthcoming (University of Santo Tomas Publishing House, Manila).

MEENA ALEXANDER was born in Allahabad, India. She lives and works in New York City, where she is Distinguished Professor of English, Hunter College/Graduate Center, CUNY. Her most recent volume of poems is *Birthplace with Buried Stones* (TriQuarterly Books/Northwestern University Press, 2013).

MAYA ABU AL-HAYAT is a Palestinian novelist, poet and author of children's books. She lives in Jerusalem.

MUHAMAD TAWFIQ ALI is a linguist, literary critic and translator of English, Arabic and Kurdish (Sorani), in any combination. He is a Member of the Chartered Institute of Linguistics. He lives in Essex, England.

DAVID HOPFFER ALMADA served as Minister of Culture and Information of Cabo Verde from 1986 to 1991 and is former Minister of Justice. Mr. Almada is a lawyer and resides on the island of Santiago, Cabo Verde.

MARK ANDRYCZYK is the administrator of the Ukrainian Studies Program and lecturer in Ukrainian literature at the Department of Slavic Languages and Literatures at Columbia University. He is an active translator of contemporary Ukrainian literature into English.

BROTHER ANTHONY was born in Cornwall (United Kingdom) in 1942. A member of the Community of Taizé, he has lived in the Republic of Korea since 1980. He is a chair-professor of Dankook University, Seoul. He has published some 30 volumes of translations of Korean poetry and fiction into English, including eight volumes by Ko Un.

NORA ATALLA is of Greek-Lebanese and Franco-Georgian origin. She is a poet, novelist and short story writer. She was a finalist for the 2014 Alain-Grandbois Prize of the Académie des lettres du Québec for her poetry collection, *Hommes de sable*. She lives between Morocco and Québec.

GABEBA BADEROON is a South African poet, and the author of the collections *The Dream in the Next Body*, *The Museum of Ordinary Life* and *A Hundred Silences*. A literary scholar, she is the author of *Regarding Muslims: from Slavery to Post-apartheid* (Wits, 2014).

DATO BARBAKADZE (Tbilisi, Georgia) founded the literary video-magazine, *Dato Barbakadze's Magazine* in 1991 while studying at Tbilisi State University. A member of the European Writers Union, he has published more than 20 books of poetry, prose and essays in German and is widely translated.

DARA BARNAT's poetry and translations appear in, among other places, *The Cortland Review, Poet Lore, Ha'aretz, Lilith, diode*. Her collection of poems *In the Absence* is forthcoming from WordTech/Turning Point in 2016. She holds a PhD from Tel Aviv University and teaches at York College and Queens College in New York.

GUZAL BEGIM is one of the leading representatives of contemporary Uzbek poetry. Her books include *Jingle of Silence* and *Shadow of a Flying Leaf* translated into English by Rachel Harrell and Azam Abidov.

ROSEBUD BEN-ONI is a CantoMundo Fellow and a recipient of the 2014 NYFA Fellowship in Poetry. Her work has appeared in, among other places, *Poetry* and *The American Poetry Review*. She is the author of *Solecism* and an editorial advisor for VIDA: Women in Literary Arts.

MUTALIP BEPPAYEV is considered the first Balkar poet to write in free verse. In 2012 he was awarded the Makhmudi Kashgarsky International Award in Ankara for the story "Fugitive". He is the first Russian to be given this award.

REI BERROA, born in Santiago, Dominican Republic, is a poet, activist, university professor, literary critic, and musician. He has published more than 40 books of poetry, anthologies, and literary criticism.

ZOFIA BESZCZYNSKA is a poet, author of fantasy tales for adults and children, and book reviewer. She has been a scholar of the Children's Library in Munich and the Baltic Centre for Writers and Translators in Visby, and an editor of *Nowe Książki* (New Books). In 2013, she was awarded the annual medal of the Polish IBBY Section for her children's writing.

JUDITH BEVERIDGE is the author of six volumes of poetry, most recently *Devadatta's Poems* (Giramondo) and *Hook and Eye* (George Braziller). She is the poetry editor of *Meanjin* and teaches creative writing at the University of Sydney, Australia.

GOVINDA RAJ BHATTARAI is Professor of English Literature at Tribhuwan University in Kathmandu, Nepal. In addition to his translations, he has written several novels, essay anthologies and several works of criticism. His contribution to reshaping and reforming Nepalese literature is well-acknowledged.

SHEENA BLACKHALL is a prolific Scottish poet, ballad singer and storyteller. In 2009 she was appointed Aberdeen's first Makar (Poet Laureate). Her latest poetry collection is *The Space Between: New and Selected Poems* (Aberdeen University Press).

RICHARD BLANCO was the 2013 inaugural poet for President Barack Obama. He is the author of several books, including *Prince of Los Cocuyos: A Miami Childhood* (Ecco, 2014) and *For All of Us, One Today*.

GERNOT BLUME is a German poet, musician, composer, musicologist and educator. His work, performed throughout the world, combines multicultural improvisation and original compositions.

Born in Barbados, **KAMAU BRATHWAITE** is a co-founder of the Caribbean Artists Movement and the author of numerous collections of poetry, including *Elegguas* (2010) and the Griffin International Poetry Prize winner *Slow Horses* (2005). His awards include both fellowships and literary prizes. He lives in Barbados and New York City.

ABENA P.A. BUSIA was born in Ghana. She is the current Chair of the Department of Women's and Gender Studies at Rutgers University, New Brunswick, N.J. She is the author of two poetry collections, *Testimonies of Exile* (1990) and *Traces of a Life* (2008).

ROBERT CHANDLER has translated the works of such Russian writers as Alexander Pushkin, Vasily Grossman and Andrey Platonov. He has compiled two anthologies of Russian short stories and Russian magic tales. A third anthology, *The Penguin Book of Russian Poetry*, was published in February 2015.

VIKA CHEMBARTSEVA is a poet, writer and translator. Honors include the "Silver Sagittarius" international literary award (Los Angeles, 2010) and first place in the fifth international "Wind of Wanderings" competition for young Russian poets abroad (Rome, 2012).

LYN COFFIN is a widely published and award-winning American writer of fiction. She is also a non-fiction writer, playwright, editor and translator. She is the author of 15 books, including four books of poetry and nine translations.

BELLE CUSHING is an American translator and writer based in New York. She specializes in French and Italian contemporary poetry, but also in food writing.

KWAME DAWES, who was born in Ghana, is the author of 19 books of poetry and numerous other books of fiction, criticism, and essays. His latest collection is *Duppy Conqueror: New and Selected Poems* (Copper Canyon, 2013). He is an educator, editor of *Prairie Schooner*, and the Artistic Director of the Calabash International Literary Festival.

ALESSANDRO DE FRANCESCO is an internationally recognized Italian poet, artist and essayist currently based in Brussels, Belgium.

CAROLINA DE ROBERTIS is an award-winning, internationally bestselling author of three novels, including *The Gods of Tango*. Her work has been translated into 16 languages. She is the translator of novels by Alejandro Zambra and Roberto Ampuero.

JEAN DÉSY is a widely published poet. He is the recipient of the 2010 Prix des Écrivains francophones d'Amérique for his poem "Toundra/ Tundra". His most recent collection of poetry is *Isuma: anthologie de poésie nordique* (Mémoire d'encrier, 2013). He is also an M.D. who has been practicing medicine in the North of Québec since 1978.

SHARON DOLIN (New York City) is the author of five poetry books, most recently, *Whirlwind* and *Burn and Dodge*, and winner of the AWP Donald Hall Prize in Poetry. She teaches at the 92nd Street Y and directs the poetry workshop "Writing About Art in Barcelona".

TISHANI DOSHI is a poet, novelist, and dancer. Her latest book is *Fountainville*, a medieval Welsh tale recast among opium dens, gang wars, and a surrogacy clinic. She lives in Tamil Nadu, India.

MARK DOTY's *Fire to Fire: New and Selected Poems* (Harper Perennial, 2008) was awarded the National Book Award for Poetry. He is the author of nine books of poems and five volumes of non-fiction prose. He lives in New York City and is Distinguished Professor at Rutgers University. A new collection, *Deep Lane*, is forthcoming from W.W. Norton in 2015.

JONATHAN DUNNE was born in Kingston-upon-Thames, England, and studied Classics at Oxford University. He is director of the publishing house Small Stations Press. He translates from Bulgarian, Catalan, Galician and Spanish into English.

TSVETANKA ELENKOVA (Sofia, Bulgaria) is a poet, essayist and editor. She has published four poetry books, two of which have been translated into English: *The Seventh Gesture* (2010) and *Crookedness* (2013). She is the editor of an anthology of Bulgarian poetry in English, *At the End of the World: Contemporary Poetry from Bulgaria* (2012).

MENNA ELFYN is a Welsh poet who has published over 20 books and whose work has been translated into over 20 languages. She is President of Wales PEN Cymru and Director of the Masters Programme in Creative Writing at Trinity University, Carmarthen.

AMIRA EL-ZEIN is a Lebanonese poet and translator whose work has been published in English, French and Arabic. She is the author of the monograph "Islam, Arabs, and the Intelligent World of the Jinn", as well as numerous other journal articles. She teaches at Georgetown University in Qatar.

JULIA ENRIQUEZ (Rosario, Argentina) is a poet and translator, who is also director of the publishing house Danke. She is currently studying Philosophy at the National University of Rosario.

YURY ENTIN is a Russian playwright and poet. Several hundred of his verses have been set to music in films and animated movies. He is widely known in the Russian Federation and the republics of the former Soviet Union.

ALISON ENTREKIN is a literary translator from the Portuguese. Her translations include *City of God* by Paulo Lins, *The Eternal Son* by Cristovão Tezza, *Near to the Wild Heart* by Clarice Lispector, *Budapest* by Chico Buarque and *Crow Blue* by Adriana Lisboa.

MARJORIE EVASCO is an award-winning Filipino poet. She has won many awards, including the National Book Awards from the Manila Critics' Circle for poetry, oral history and art. Her work appears in *Language for a New Century: Poems from Asia, the Middle East and Beyond* (Norton, 2010).

PETER FALLON, founder of The Gallery Press, was born in Germany and grew up near Kells in County Meath. He is an Honours Graduate of Trinity College, Dublin, where he has been Writer Fellow and Visiting Writer in the English Department.

LAURENT FELS was born in Esch-sur-Alzette, Luxembourg. He is a writer and a professor of French literature in the Grand Duchy of Luxembourg.

TESS GALLAGHER is the author of eight volumes of poetry, including *Midnight Lantern: New and Selected Poems*, *Dear Ghosts*, and *Moon Crossing Bridge*, all from Graywolf Press.

MIMI HACHIKAI is a Japanese poet and writer. A recipient of the Nakahara Chuya Prize and the Geijutsu Sensho Shinjin Prize, she has published several anthologies, including *The Quickening Field*, *The Night Those Who Eat Get Eaten*, and *The Hiding Leaf*. She is Visiting Professor in Literature, Waseda University.

JOUMANA HADDAD is a Lebanese poet, journalist and activist for human rights in the Arab world. Her books have been translated into more than 15 languages. For her cultural and social activism, in March 2014, *CEO Middle East* magazine selected her as one of the world's ten most powerful Arab women.

ANJUM HASAN is a novelist and poet. She is the books editor at *The Caravan* magazine, and lives in Bangalore, India.

ÁNGELA HERNÁNDEZ NÚÑEZ (Dominican Republic) is a writer and poet. She is the former editor of the literary magazine *Xinesquema*, and a Member of the Dominican Academy of Language. Her work has been translated into numerous languages and appears in close to 100 anthologies.

JUAN FELIPE HERRERA, poet and author of children's books and others in various genres, teaches creative writing at the University of California in Riverside. In 2012, he was appointed by Governor Jerry Brown as the Poet Laureate of California. His new book is *Portraits of Hispanic American Heroes*.

KIRSTEN HOLMES (South Africa) was taught all she knows about poetry by Lionel Abrahams. Her first poetry collection, *Stick Figures*, was published in 2011. She is currently working on her her first novel, *The Gospel of the Snail*, and on her second poetry collection.

ELIN AP HYWEL (Wales) is a poet, editor and translator. She currently does free-lance work, including translations from Welsh into English. Her writing has appeared in numerous anthologies, and her books of poetry include: *Pethau Brau (Delicate Things)*, and *Ffiniau* (Borders).

SERGIO INFANTE (Santiago, Chile) has published numerous collections of poetry, including: *Abismos grises* (Gray Abysses,1967), *Retrato de época* (Portrait of an Era,1982), *La del alba sería* (*Day was Dawning*, 2002) and *Las aguas bisiestas* (*The Leap Waters*, 2012). His poetry has also appeared in Latin America and Europe. He has been living in Sweden since 1975.

NORBERTO JAMES has been called the "most famous living poet" of the Dominican Republic. His poems from seven published works, have been translated into three languages, and have received prestigious literary awards in the United States and the Dominican Republic.

MARIT IRENE JENSEN lives in Oslo and is also known to many Norwegians as a supporting actress in movies and on television. She writes poems, as well as novels and fairy tales.

FADY JOUDAH is a Palestinian-American poet, physician and translator. His work has received several national and international awards. His translation of Ghassan Zaqtan's *Like a Straw Bird It Follows Me* (2012) won the Griffin International Poetry Prize in 2013.

MIMI KHALVATI was born in Iran and grew up in England. She has published eight collections of poetry with Carcanet Press, including most recently, *The Weather Wheel*, a Poetry Book Society recommendation. She is a Fellow of the Royal Society of Literature.

MAHIRUHA KLEIN lives in Chicago. His favorite poets include Dylan Thomas, Yeats and Walt Whitman. His poetry is also inspired by contemporary musicians, like Mumford and Sons, whose music reflects sincere poetic depth.

YUSEF KOMUNYAKAA's books of poetry include *Warhorses*, *The Chameleon Couch*, and *Testimony, A Tribute to Charlie Parker*. His forthcoming collection, *The Emperor of Water Clocks*, will be published by Farrar, Straus and Giroux in 2015. His plays, performance art, and libretti have been performed internationally.

ANDREY KOROVIN (Russian Federation) is a poet whose work has been published in many well-known Russian literary magazines. He has organized numerous literary festivals and served as the Vice-Chairman of the Commission on Work, which represents young Russian writers.

AGNIESZKA KRECZMAR is a Polish translator of English and American literature, including the works of Edgar Allen Poe, J.R.R. Tolkien, Mark Twain. She is also a specialist in ninth-century English poetry.

DMYTRO LAZUTKIN is a Ukrainian poet whose honours include the Granoslov literary award for young writers (2002) and the Kultrevansh (Cultrevenge, 2005). In 2006 he was named Poet of the Year by PROZA digital media.

ANDRÉANA E. LEFTON is a writer, teacher and researcher. Her achievements have been widely recognized, including the Elie Wiesel Prize in Ethics and the London School of Economics Bernard Levin Award for Student Journalism. At present, she is a guest contributor at On Being, home to the Civil Conversations Project.

SOILA LEHTONEN is a journalist, theatre critic and was Editor-in-Chief of Books in Finland from 2007 to 2014. In 2000, with Hildi Hawkins, she edited *Helsinki: A Literary Companion*, a collection of writings about the city of Helsinki.

SHIRLEY GEOK-LIN LIM was born in Malaysia. She is a Commonwealth Poetry Prize winner, and has published six poetry collections, three chapbooks, three novels, and a memoir, *Among the White Moon Faces* (American Book Award).

ADRIANA LISBOA, Brazilian poet and writer of fiction, is the author of, among others, the novels *Symphony in White* (winner of the José Saramago Prize) and *Crow Blue* (an "Independent" book of the year).

HERBERT LOMAS (1924–2011) was a prize-winning British poet and translated Finnish poetry and prose for more than thirty years. His collected poems, *A Casual Knack of Living*, appeared in England in 2009.

RAQUEL LUBARTOWSKI, who also writes as Raquel Nogara, is a Uruguayan lesbian poet, novelist, and psychologist. She has received numerous awards over the decades, and wrote the script for the film *Una Bala Para el Che*.

THAKUR PRASAD MAINALI (Walting Village, Nepal) is a renowned sculptor. He is also a writer whose published works include *Samarpan* (in Nepalese) and *Flames of Devotion* (in English).

TANYA MANORI ULUWITIYA from the Dominican Republic, is a translator and researcher on post-colonial and diasporic literature.

MICHÈLE VOLTAIRE MARCELIN is a poet, writer, performer and painter who was born and raised in Haiti, sojourned in Chile, and currently lives in the United States. Among her many books of poetry and prose are *Lost and Found* and *Amours et Bagatelles* (CIDIHCA, Montréal, 2009), which was translated into Spanish by Editorial ALBA as *Amores y cosas sin importancia*.

DAVID MATEVOSSIAN (Armenia) is a producer, film director and translator of stories and poems. He is the general manager of Hrant Matevossian Cultural Benevolent Foundation, and since 2001, co-founder of the annual Literary Ark International Festival in Armenia.

KHALED MATTAWA is a poet and translator and a recipient of the MacArthur "Genius" Grant. He is an Assistant Professor of Language and Literature at the University of Michigan, and the author of the poetry volumes *Ismaila Eclipse* and *Zodiac of Echoes*.

LAREN McCLUNG is the author of a collection of poems, *Between Here and Monkey Mountain* (Sheep Meadow Press), and co-editor of a forthcoming anthology, *Inheriting the War: Poetry and Prose by Descendants of Vietnam Veterans and Refugees*. She teaches at New York University.

IMAN MERSAL (Egypt) is the author of four books of poems in Arabic: *Characterizations, A Dark Alley Suitable for Dance Lessons, Walking As Long As Possible* and *Alternative Geography*. She immigrated to Canada in 1999, where she is currently an assistant professor of Arabic at the University of Alberta.

MARY ANNE MOHANRAJ, born in Sri Lanka, is the author of *Bodies in Motion, The Stars Change*, and eleven other books. She is a Clinical Assistant Professor of English at the University of Illinois at Chicago.

NATALIA MOLEBATSI is a South African writer and performance poet. Tembisa-born and raised, Natalia has performed throughout the world and is a founding member of the South African/Italian band Soul Making.

NORA NADJARIAN (Cyprus) is a poet and short story writer. She has published three collections of poetry: *The Voice at the Top of the Stairs* (2001), *Cleft in Twain* (2003) and *25 Ways to Kiss a Man* (2004). Her work was included in Best European Fiction 2011 (Dalkey Archive Press) and in the poetry anthology *Being Human* (Bloodaxe Books, 2011).

STAS NAMIN (ANASTAS A. MIKOYAN), is a Russian musician, composer, theatre director and actor, known for *How the Beatles Rocked the Kremlin* (2009). He is the founder and leader of Russia's first national super group, *The Flowers* rock band.

NAZMUN NESA (pen name Nazmun Nesa Piari) was born in Bangladesh and lives in Berlin. She is an author, poet and international freelance journalist.

SYLVIE NICOLAS, poet and literary translator, gives public readings of her poetry and is currently pursuing a Ph.D. in creative writing and research at Laval University, Québec.

NAOMI SHIHAB NYE's most recent book is *The Turtle of Oman* (Greenwillow), named to The Horn Book's Best Books Fanfare List for 2014. She is the author of several other poetry collections, and has also written a collection of essays and a young adult novel. She lives in San Antonio, Texas.

IKEOGU OKE, is a Nigerian writer, poet and journalist. He is the author of *Where I Was Born; Salutes without Guns*, a Times Literary Supplement Book of the Year (2010); and *In the Wings of Waiting*, with a foreword by the Nobel Laureate Nadine Gordimer.

JACQUES OUELLET was born in Québec. He was awarded the Octave Crémazie prize for his 1987 collection, *Qui ose regarder*. He has published six volumes of poetry.

ZORAN PAUNOVIĆ is an English language professor on the Faculty of Philosophy, University of Novi Sad, Serbia.

VICTOR PEÑARANDA is a poet, writer-researcher and resource person on community development from the Philippines. He is the author of three literary collections: *Voyage in Dry Season* (poems), *Pilgrim in Transit* (poems), and *Lucid Lightning* (poems & prose).

EMMY PÉREZ is the author of *Solstice* (Swan Scythe Press). She is an associate professor at the University of Texas-Pan American in the Rio Grande Valley.

PASCALE PETIT has published six collections, four of which were shortlisted for the T.S. Eliot Prize and three featured as Books of the Year in the *Times Literary Supplement*, the *Observer* and the *Independent*. Her latest is T.S. Eliot-shortlisted *Fauverie* (Seren, 2014).

SILAS PINTO teaches at Tufts University in Medford, Massachusetts, in the School Psychology Graduate Program of the Department of Education. He is a composer of traditional and modern Afrocentric music and the director of New Wave Arts and the Cabo Verdean and Brazilian Cultural Center of Rhode Island.

MICHEL PLEAU lives in his hometown, Québec City. He won the Governor General's Award for poetry in 2008 for *La lenteur du monde (Eternity Taking Its Time)*. He is Canada's new parliamentary poet laureate (2014-2016).

RAKSHAT PURI (1924–2012) was a renowned journalist, writer and poet from New Delhi.

SHAZEA QURAISHI is a Pakistani-born Canadian poet, play-wright and translator based in London, where she teaches creative writing.

MARGARET RANDALL, born in New York City, is a feminist poet, writer, photographer and social activist. She is the author of more than 80 books, published in many different countries.

SHIRIN RAZAVIAN is a Tehran-born British poet whose work has appeared in *Poetry London, The London Magazine, Exiled Writers Magazine*, and *Persian Book Review*, among others. She has published Farsi and English poetry collections in the UK, the latest being *Which Shade of Blue* (2010).

LJUBIVOJE RŠUMOVIĆ is a Serbian poet, novelist, and playwright. He has worked for Belgrade Radio-Television, for *Književne novine* and for the children's theatre, Boško Buha. His 85 books include works for both children and adults. In 1996, he received a UNESCO award for his book, *The Primer of Children's Rights*.

BREDA WALL RYAN lives in Bray, County Wicklow, Ireland. Her fiction and poetry have been widely published in journals and anthologies. She has won numerous awards, most recently The Gregory O'Donoghue International Poetry Competition. Her collection, *In a Hare's Eye*, is forthcoming by Doire Press in March 2015.

LEE SANG-WHA is an emeritus professor at Chung-Ang University, Republic of Korea, specializing in modern English novels and utopian ideas in literature. She has translated ten books, both into Korean, including Gary Snyder's prose works, and into English, including volumes of Ko Un's poetry.

JEAN-FRANÇOIS SENÉ retired after an academic career. In addition to his work as a translator, he has published several volumes of his own poetry.

IGOR SHAFERAN (1932-1994) was a well known Russian poet and author of song verses for animated and children's films. His poem "We wish you happiness..." was set to music by Stas Namin, and is as popular in Russia as the songs of the Beatles in the West.

Mumbai-based **SUNIL SHARMA**, a college principal, is also a widely published bilingual Indian critic, poet, literary inter-viewer, editor, translator, essayist and fiction writer. He is a re-cipient of the UK-based Destiny Poets' inaugural Poet of the Year award (2012).

ADAM J. SORKIN is an award-winning translator of more than 50 books of contemporary Romanian poetry. He is Dis-tinguished Professor of English at Penn State Brandywine, in Media, Pennsylvania.

ALAN SPENCE is an award-winning Scottish poet and play-wright, novelist and short story writer. He is a Professor in Creative Writing at the University of Aberdeen. His most recent book is a novel, *Night Boat* (Canongate), and his most recent poetry collection is *Morning Glory* (Renaissance Press).

GRETA STODDART was born in England and grew up in Belgium and Oxford. She studied drama, touring the UK, Europe and South America with a theater company for five years. She has published three books of poetry and has won the Geoffrey Faber Memorial Prize.

TAMARA A. STRUGO was born in Mendoza, Argentina, where she studied English and English Literature. She currently teaches Spanish at Stockholm University in Sweden.

LUCIJA STUPICA is a Slovenian poet and interior designer. Her first book of poetry, *Čelo na soncu (Forehead in the Sun)*, won the seventeenth Slovenian Book Fair Award for the best first book, as well as the Zlata Ptica (Golden Bird) award for the best artistic achievments. She lives in Sweden.

HARASHITA SUNAOSHI is a sociolinguist specializing in intercultural communication. She teaches at several universities in Tokyo, including the School of Law, Waseda University.

GEORGE SZIRTES is a poet and translator. Born in Hungary, he came to England in 1956. He writes in English and translates from Hungarian into English. His many books of poetry have won the T.S. Eliot Prize, the Faber Memorial Prize and others.

ILPO TIIHONEN is a Finnish poet, playwright and translator whose first collection was published in 1975. Playing masterfully with words and rhyme, he often creates ironically slanted lyrical satire.

MARK TREDINNICK is an Australian poet and nature writer. His 14 works of poetry and prose include *Bluewren Cantos, Fire Diary, Almost Everything I Know, The Blue Plateau*, and *The Little Red Writing Book*. He is the father of five and lives in Newcastle, on the east coast of Australia.

KO UN is a distinguished Korean poet. He has published 155 books, including the monumental 30-volume *Maninbo (Ten Thousand Lives)*, with 4,001 poems, and the 7-volume epic

Mount Baekdu. His works have been translated into more than 25 languages.

PRISCILA UPPAL is a Canadian poet, fiction writer, memoirist, playwright, and Professor of English at York University. Her books have been published internationally and translated into numerous languages. *Time Out London* dubbed her "Canada's coolest poet".

LILIANA URSU is a well-known Romanian poet whose publications in English include *Goldsmith Market* (Zephyr, 2003) and *Lightwall* (Zephyr, 2009). She holds the rank of Knight of Arts and Literature, Romania's highest national cultural honour. Her collection, *A Path to the Sea* (Pleasure Boat Studio, 2011), won the Silver Award in poetry, ForeWord Reviews Book of the Year, 2011.

SIDURI URUK is the author's pen name. She is an Iraqi journalist who also writes on political issues.

ELIZABETH WELLINGTON is married to the Dominican poet, Norberto James, and has published numerous translations of his poems as well as short stories by Dominican authors. She is currently writing fiction.

NILPUSHPI WHITE, Canadian-born, lives in New York and has embraced an international perspective while working as an editorial associate at the United Nations. Her poems and stories reflect her worldwide travel experiences and deep interest in yoga and meditation.

JEFFREY YANG is the author of the poetry collections *Vanishing-Line* and *An Aquarium*. His translations include Ahmatjan Osman's *Uyghurland, the Farthest Exile*, which will be published in Spring 2015. He works as an editor at New Directions Publishing and New York Review Books.

NIHAL YEĞİNOBALI lives in Turkey and is a well-known translator of fiction, specializing in English classical translation from English to Turkish. She studied English literature at New York University.

YEVGENY YEVTUSHENKO is a Russian poet, writer, actor

and film director who is best known for his poem "Babi Yar" and his collaboration with composer Dmitri Shostakovich. One of the most famous poets of the 1950s and 1960s, Yevtushenko made an important contribution to promoting progress, openness, human rights and freedoms in the former Soviet Union.

SAADI YOUSSEF (Iraq) is considered one of the most important contemporary poets in the Arab world. Following his experience as a political prisoner in Iraq, he worked as a journalist throughout North Africa and the Middle East. He is also a leading translator of English literature into Arabic, and now lives in London.

JAVIER ZAMORA (El Salvador) migrated to the United States at the age of nine. He is a prize-winning poet whose work has been featured in *Best New Poets 2013*, and elsewhere in print and online. Honors include an NEA fellowship and the Olive B. O'Connor Fellowship from Colgate University.

DI ZOU was born in China and lives in New York. She is a translator at the United Nations and a member of the United Nations SRC Society of Writers.

The United Nations Staff Recreation Council Society of Writers seeks to promote the written word as a powerful and artistic means of expression. The Society publishes an international literary magazine, *Reflections*, and sponsors literary events throughout the year.

Members of the Society include poets, essayists, writers of fiction and journalists from the international community, including serving and retired United Nations staff members and their relatives, as well as representatives of the diplomatic corps and non-governmental organizations.

The UNSRC Society of Writers offers special programmes to the international community at United Nations Headquarters in New York to stimulate thought and to promote dialogue. Many of these programmes celebrate individual artistic endeavours. These have included *Can Poetry Save the Earth?*, a programme in honour of the United Nations Conference on Sustainable Development (Rio+20) and National Poetry Month (April 2012), and *A Tribute and Celebration on the occasion of the birthday of Chinua Achebe* (November 2013).

CREDITS

All poems copyright of and reprinted with permission of the authors, with the following acknowledgements:

Maya Abu Al-Hayat – "Distance", translation from Arabic by Fady Joudah, previously published in *That Smile, That Heart* (Dar Raya Publishing House, Haifa, 2013).

Adonis – "Tomorrow", translation from Arabic by Khaled Mattawa, reprinted from *Adonis: Selected Poems* (Yale University Press, 2010) by permission of the author and the publisher.

Jim Pascual Agustin – "Puddles after the First Monsoon Rain", previously published in *Alien to Any Skin* (Manila, UST Publishing House, 2011).

Meena Alexander – "Water Table", from *Illiterate Heart*. Copyright © 2002 by Meena Alexander. Published by TriQuarterly Books/Northwestern University Press (2002). All rights reserved.

David Hopffer Almada – "Um Dia Feliz" / "A Happy Day", previously published in *Cabo Verde de Esperança Mandela No Céu!*

Gabeba Baderoon – "Primal Scene", previously published in *A Hundred Silences* (Kwela/Snailpress, 2006).

Dato Barbakadze - "After Bad Weather" previously published in *Still Life With Snow and Other Poems* (Bedouin Books, Port Townsend, 2014).

Rosebud Ben-Oni – "A Poem for My Niece on No Particular Day", previously published in *Solecism* (Virtual Artists' Collective, 2013).

Rei Berroa – "Utilidades de la risa" / "The Usefulness of Laughter", previously published in *Libro de los dones y los bienes* (Caracas, 2010; Monterrey, México, 2013).

Zofia Beszczynska – "nagła chwila wiatła" / "a sudden moment of light", previously published in *miejsca magiczne* (magic places), Warsaw, Nowy Świat, 2003.

Judith Beveridge – "The Fishermen", previously published in *Accidental Grace*, University of Queensland Press, St. Lucia, Queensland, 1996.

Sheena Blackhall – "A Buddhist Valentine", previously published in *The Space Between: New & Selected Poems* (Aberdeen, Aberdeen University Press, 2014).

Richard Blanco – "Hoy, Uno" / "One Today", previously published in *For All of Us, One Today* (Beacon Press, 2013), and in *One Today* (University of Pittsburgh Press, 2013), reprinted in English by permission of the author and the publisher.

Abena P.A. Busia – "A Wedding Song", previously published in *Traces of a Life* (Ayebia Clarke Publishing, Ltd., 2008) by permission of the author and the publisher.

Sri Chinmoy - "The Roots of Delight-Tree", previously published in *Ten Thousand Flower-Flames*, Part 33 (Agni Press, 1982); and "Sada Susanga Hiya Bihanga", previously published in *Pole-Star Promise-Light*, Part 1 (Agni Press, 1975), Copyright © Sri Chinmoy Centre.

Alessandro De Francesco – "stiamo sospesi sugli scalini" / "we are suspended on the stairs", from "The End (An Agenda)", translation from Italian by Belle Cushing. Previously published in the online journal *Continent*.

Jean Désy – "Dans une tente dans la toundra" / "In a Tent on the Tundra", in *Toundra/Tundra*, Xyz Publishing, Montréal, 2009.

Sharon Dolin – "If Happiness Is Luck", reprinted from *Whirlwind* (University of Pittsburgh Press, 2012) by permission of the author and the publisher.

Tsvetanka Elenkova – "Cherni Vrah", translation from Bulgarian by Jonathan Dunne, previously published in *Sedmiyat jest*, Zaharii Stoyanov, Sofia, 2005; and *The Seventh Gesture*, Shearsman Books, Exeter, 2010.

Menna Elfyn - "Cerdd garegog" /"Stones", previously published in *Perffaith Nam/Perfect Blemish: New & Selected Poems 1995-2007*, Bloodaxe Books, Welsh-English Bilingual Edition.

Julia Enriquez – "Me dijeron que debía asumir por mi cuenta el lenguaje entero" / "They told me I had to take over language all by myself", from *Ambulancia improvisada / Improvised Ambulance* (2014).

Peter Fallon – "Day and Night", previously published in *The Company of Horses* (The Gallery Press, 2007).

Laurent Fels – "au carrefour de la solitude" / "at the crossroads of solitude", translation from French by Jean-François Sené. Previously published in *Regards de Soie – Silky Gazes*, by Poiêtês Editions (Luxembourg).

Anjum Hasan – "In My Mother's Clothes", previously published in Anjum Hasan, *Street on the Hill* (Sahitya Akademi, New Delhi: 2006).

Sergio Infante – "La dicha" / "Bliss", translated from Spanish by Tamara A. Strugo, previously published in *Las aguas bisiestas*, Editorial Catalonia, Santiago de Chile, 2012.

Norberto James – "(Re)posesión" / "(Re)posession", previously published in *La urdimbre del silencio*, Consejo Presidencial de

in the literary journal *Books from Finland*, March 2007.

Priscila Uppal – "Good Things", previously published in *Pretending to Die* (Exile Editions 2001).

Liliana Ursu – "Îmbătrânind" / "Growing Old", previously published in *A Path to the Sea*, translation from Romanian by Adam J. Sorkin, Liliana Ursu, and Tess Gallagher. New York: Pleasure Boat Studio, 2011.

Siduri Uruk – "An Iraqi Girl's Dream of a Bridegroom" (English title) / "The Personnel Specifications of a Bridegroom as the Wishes of Every Iraqi Bride" (Arabic title), translated from Arabic by Muhamad Tawfiq Ali, previously published online, http://www.kitabat.com (28 July 2007). Reprinted by permission of Muhamad Tawfiq Ali.

Jeffrey Yang – "What Is", previously published in Academy of American Poets/*Poem-A-Day*.

Saadi Youssef – "Happiness", translation from Arabic by Khaled Mattawa, previously published in Saadi Youssef, *Without an Alphabet, Without a Face: Selected Poems*. Tr. Khaled Mattawa, Graywolf Press, 2003.

Javier Zamora – "Si Fuera" / "If It Were", forthcoming in *Ghost-Fishing: An Eco-Justice Poetry Anthology*.

The editors have made every effort to locate all rights holders and obtain the necessary permissions for reprinting. Any omissions are wholly unintentional; forgiveness is requested.

To see the complete list of Member States according to their regional groupings, please refer to the website of the General Assembly:http://www.un.org/depts/DGACM/RegionalGroups.shtml.